a WEE GUIDE to
the Castles *and*
Mansions *of* Scotland

A GUIDE TO 147 CASTLES, PALACES,
MANSIONS AND HISTORIC
HOUSES OPEN TO THE PUBLIC

Martin Coventry

GOBLINSHEAD

Edinburgh

...nsions of Scotland

First Published 1998
© Martin Coventry 1998
Published by GOBLINSHEAD
12 Merchiston Crescent
Edinburgh EH10 5AS
Scotland

British Library Cataloguing in Publication Data
A catalogue record for this book is available from the British Library.

ISBN 1 899874 11 9

Typeset by GOBLINSHEAD using Desktop Publishing
Typeset in Garamond Narrow

WEE GUIDES
Scottish History
William Wallace
Haunted Castles of Scotland
Mary, Queen of Scots
Robert the Bruce
Robert Burns
The Picts
The Castles and Mansions of Scotland
Old Churches and Abbeys of Scotland
The Jacobites
Malt Whisky

a **WEE GUIDE** *to*
the Castles *and*
Mansions *of* Scotland

A GUIDE TO 147 CASTLES, PALACES,
MANSIONS AND HISTORIC
HOUSES OPEN TO THE PUBLIC

Contents

List of illustrations

Introduction

In this small book I have tried to include as many castles and mansions regularly open to the public as possible, restricting myself to those that I believe are worth a visit. I have not, however, restricted entries to castles – or in any event, buildings with the word 'castle' in their name – but have included fortresses, tower houses, mansions, historic houses, palaces, and the odd fort, barracks and motte. Some of the sites will take only a short time to visit, while others could take much of the day.

It should be said that this wee book owes much to its older, larger and more expensive brother *The Castles of Scotland* 2E, although that work does not include mansion houses. I have tried to include such information as I find interesting, concentrating on history and facilities. After all, the visitor will find out all about the physical description and location of the site by visiting it – which is often most of the fun. There are also 50 or so additional sites near the end of the book.

If intending to visit many of the sites in this book, it is worth considering joining both the Friends of Historic Scotland and The National Trust for Scotland. Benefits include – for a fee – free entry to properties in Scotland, free or reduced entry fees to properties in the rest of Britain, as well as a quarterly magazine, reduction of the price of merchandise, and other offers. Historic Scotland can be reached on 0131 668 8800 and The National Trust for Scotland on 0131 226 5922.

Finally, I hope the reader gets as much enjoyment from visiting the fascinating buildings covered in the following pages as much as I have.

Thanks to all the castle owners and administrators who responded to queries so quickly by post or over the phone. Thanks also to Joyce Miller, who had to read over another book about castles, and all those at Goblinshead.

MC, Edinburgh, February 1998

How to use this book

This book is divided into two main parts:

- The first part (pages 1-9) is an overview of the development of castles and mansions in Scotland.
- The second part (pages 10-85) lists 147 castles, palaces, historic houses and mansions which are open to the public. The section begins with a list of places in the book (page 10-11), which should be used in conjunction with the map (pages 12-13) which locates every site. The gazetteer is listed alphabetically (from page 15). Each entry begins with the name of the castle or mansion, its location, then its National Grid Reference and Ordnance Sheet Landranger number, as well as the reference to the map (pages 12-13). Also included is the owner: Historic Scotland (HS); National Trust for Scotland (NTS); privately owned/local authority (Pri/LA). This is followed by a description of the site, with attractions and disabled facilities. The final part covers opening with telephone numbers and facilities, including parking (P), refreshments (R), sales area (S), admission charge (£), WC (WC). Fifty further buildings or gardens open to the public are listed (page 86) with telephone numbers and brief details on opening. A glossary of terms (pages 87) concludes this section.

An index (pages 88-90) lists all the sites, people and events alphabetically, and includes many cross-references.

Warning

While the information in this book was believed to be correct at time of going to press – and was checked with the visitor attractions or their advertising material – opening times and facilities, or other information, may differ from that included. All information should be checked before embarking on any visit. Inclusion in the text is no indication that a site is open to the public or that it should be visited. Many sites, particularly ruins, are potentially dangerous and great care should be taken: the publisher and author cannot accept responsibility for damage or injury caused from any visit.

Locations on the map are approximate. Shetland is not just off the coast of north-east Scotland, as indicated on the map, but north-east of Orkney. Apologies to Shetlanders.

The castle and mansion in Scotland

The main function of the castle was primarily defensive: to protect the lord and his family from their enemies, but in as comfortable surroundings as possible. The castle was the centre of administration, from where tenure, economy and trade were controlled, law dispensed, and wrongdoers punished. Originally a large stronghold could defend against an invading army, but by the 16th century the increased use of effective artillery pieces made castles redundant as major strong-points. As times became more peaceful, the defensive capabilities were not necessary, and many castles were abandoned for comfortable and spacious mansions, or were extended by wings and ranges of buildings.

Motte and Bailey Castles (12th century)

During the 12th century, motte and bailey castles were introduced along with feudalism into Scotland, mostly into Lowland areas. Motte and bailey castles are mostly concentrated in Clydesdale, Galloway and Grampian. There appear to have been few in central Scotland, Lothians, the north-west and the Highlands.

These castles consisted of an earthen mound, known as a motte, and a courtyard, or bailey, enclosed by a wooden palisade and defended by a ditch. The plan of the motte was usually round, but some were also oval

Duffus Castle – see next page.

1

or rectangular. At the base of the motte was a dry or wet ditch or moat.

A wooden tower was built on the motte, where the lord and his followers could shelter if attacked. The bailey contained many buildings, such as the hall, chapel, kitchen, bakehouse and stables. Wooden castles were not used for long, as they could be set alight, but had the advantage of being easy and quick to build.

Often all that remains today is evidence of the earthworks, some good examples of these being Motte of Urr, Peel Ring of Lumphanan and Doune of Invernochty. Duffus and Rothesay are two of the few examples where a stone keep was added. Other mottes and their surrounding earthworks were reused by later castle builders.

Stone Castles (12th century-)

Stone castles were built from the 12th century in Scotland, although stone-built duns and brochs – stone enclosures or round towers – had been used since before the birth of Christ.

The simplest form was a wall enclosing a two-storey hall block of wood or stone. The entrance to the hall block was on the first floor, and was reached by a ladder, which could be removed easily during attack. The wall was usually surrounded by a ditch and rampart.

Good examples of early castles include Castle Sween and Old Castle of Wick.

Bothwell Castle – see next page.

By the 13th century, walls were heightened and strengthened, enclosing a courtyard which contained both the hall and lord's chamber, as well as kitchens, bakeries, brewhouses, stables and storerooms. Corner towers were added to defend the castle. The walls were pierced by slits through which crossbows could be fired. Castles dating at least in part from this time include Balvenie, Crookston, Duart, Dundonald, Dunstaffnage, Inverlochy, Loch Doon, Skipness and Urquhart.

Strong gatehouses were added with portcullises, drawbridges, iron-studded doors, and murder-holes. The curtain walls were given battlements for archers to shelter behind. By the 14th century, large stone castles such as Bothwell, Caerlaverock and Kildrummy had been built. These consisted of a keep – a large strong tower with a hall and chambers for the lord – and thick curtain walls with round or square corner towers.

There are relatively few very large castles left in Scotland, partly due to the expense of constructing and maintaining such buildings, and partly because many were destroyed by the Scots during the Wars of Independence. Strong royal castles were maintained, including those at Edinburgh, Stirling, Dumbarton, Roxburgh and Dunbar – although little remains of the last two. A few of the most powerful families could also afford massive fortresses, such as the Douglas strongholds of Tantallon and Threave, and the Keith stronghold of Dunnottar.

Keeps (14th/15th century)

These castles consisted of a square or rectangular tower and an adjoining courtyard. The walls of the keep were thick, and normally rose through at least three storeys to a flush crenellated parapet. The basement and first floor were vaulted to increase the strength of the building. The size of the keep depended on the wealth of the builder.

The basement contained a cellar, often with no connection to the floor above. The hall was on the first floor, with a private chamber for the lord on the floor above, and a garret storey above this. The thick walls contained many mural chambers, either small bedrooms or garderobes. The entrance was at first-floor level, and was reached by an external stair. Stairs led up, within the walls, to each floor. The keep was roofed with stone slates, or slabs, to protect it against attack by fire.

The courtyard enclosed buildings such as a kitchen, stables, chapel,

Kilchurn Castle

brewhouse, and was surrounded by a wall often with a ditch and drawbridge.

Large castles which date substantially from this period are numerous – although most have been altered or extended in later centuries – and include Aberdour, Alloa, Balgonie, Cardoness, Castle Campbell, Castle Stalker, Cawdor, Craigmillar, Crichton, Delgatie, Doune, Drummond, Dunrobin, Dunvegan, Eilean Donan, Glamis, Hermitage, Huntingtower, Huntly, Kilchurn, Kilravock, Lennoxlove, Lochleven, Neidpath, Newark, Ravenscraig, Spynie and Tolquhon. Simpler castles of the period include Orchardton and Smailholm.

Palaces (15th-17th century)
The Stewart monarchs built or remodelled the royal palaces in the Renaissance style at Stirling, Holyrood, Linlithgow, Falkland and Dunfermline, creating comfortable residences preferable to royal castles.

Tower Houses (16th-17th century)
In 1535 an Act of Parliament declared that every landed man that had land valued at £100 (Scots) was to build a tower or castle to defend his lands.

Although there is no clear divide, tower houses evolved from keeps, more consideration being taken of comfort. The walls became less thick,

Cardoness Castle – see previous page.

and the entrance was moved to the basement. Parapets were corbelled-out so that they would overhang the wall and missiles could be dropped on attackers below. The corners had open rounds, and the stair was crowned by a caphouse and watch-chamber. Gunloops and shot-holes replaced arrowslits. The walls were harled and often whitewashed. Castles from this period include Aikwood, Broughty,

Smailholm Tower – see previous page.

Corgarff, Craignethan, Hollows and Lauriston.

L-plan Tower Houses (mid 16th/17th century)

The L-plan tower house had a stair-wing added to the main block. The stair was usually turnpike, and climbed only to the hall on the first floor. The upper floors were reached by a turnpike stair in a small stair-turret corbelled out, above first-floor level, in the re-entrant angle. This stair was crowned by a caphouse and watch-chamber. In some cases, the wing contained a stair which climbed to all floors, and sometimes a separate stair-tower stood within the re-entrant angle, and the wing contained chambers.

The defensive features became less obvious. Larger windows were still protected by iron yetts or grills, and gunloops became ornamental. Open rounds were replaced by bartizans, with conical roofs, and parapets were covered. Decorative features, as well as heraldic panels, inscribed lintels, tempera painting and modelled plaster work were introduced. These design features showed French and Italian influences. The tower usually had a small courtyard with ranges of buildings, including a brewhouse, stabling and more accommodation. Often there was a terraced or walled garden.

The basement was vaulted and contained a kitchen, with a large fireplace; a wine-cellar, with a small stair to the hall above; and other cellars. The hall was on the first floor of the main block with private chambers, on the floors above, and within the garret or attic storey.

Examples of L-plan towers include Balvaird, Barcaldine, Braemar, Crathes, Drumcoltran, Drumlanrig's Tower, Edzell, Greenknowe, Kellie, Scalloway and Scotstarvit.

Z-plan Tower Houses (late 16th/17th century)

Z-plan tower houses consisted of a main block, with two towers at diagonally opposite corners. One of the towers usually housed a stair, while the other provided more accommodation. Often further wings or ranges were added to the tower making it E-plan. Castles substantially from this period include Ballindalloch, Brodie, Castle Fraser, Castle Menzies, Claypotts, Elcho, Glenbuchat, Leith Hall, MacLellan's, Maxwelton and Noltland.

Elcho Castle

Forts (16th/17th/18th century)

With the advent of more sophisticated artillery, the castle became increasingly redundant as a major defensive structure. As early as the 1540s, forts were being built to withstand attack by cannon. The English constructed forts, during the invasion of Scotland in 1547-50, including those at Roxburgh, Eyemouth and Haddington, which consisted of ramparts and bastions of earth rather than high walls. In the 1650s Cromwell built forts or Citadels, such as those at Ayr, Leith, Perth, Inverlochy, Inverness and Aberdeen. The Hanoverian Government built forts, barracks and roads because of the Jacobite Risings of 1715 and 1745, including those at Fort George, Fort William, Fort Augustus and Ruthven Barracks. Other castles such as Corgarff and Braemar were remodelled with star-shaped outworks.

Mansion Houses

Even before the Jacobite Risings, most new houses had ceased to be fortified, including mansions such as Drumlanrig and Hopetoun House. By the mid 18th century, most new houses, or extensions to existing buildings, were built in a classical or symmetrical style, designed by architects such as William Adam, and his sons Robert and John. These featured pillars and pillasters, pediments and statues, fine plasterwork and interiors. Many castles were abandoned at this time, because they were cramped, uncomfortable and unfashionable. Gardens became more ornate and elaborate, and houses were surrounded by acres of parkland. Fine buildings of this period include Mellerstain, Floors, Culzean and Duff House.

Duff House

Largely as a result of Sir Walter Scott reviving interest in a romanticised Scottish past, baronial mansions came into fashion during the 19th century, incorporating or recreating mock castellated features, such as towers and turrets, corbelling and machiolations. Castles were reused, restored, reoccupied, remodelled or recreated by architects such as William Burn, James Gillespie Graham and David Bryce in the 19th century, and Sir Robert Lorimer in the 20th century. Buildings dating from the 19th and 20th centuries include Armadale, Ayton, Balmoral (holiday home of the Royal family), Blairquhan, Fasque House, Mount Stuart House, Scone Palace and Torosay; while buildings which were remodelled and/or extended include Blair, Bowhill, Brodick, Drum, Dunrobin, Dunvegan, and Lauriston.

Dunrobin Castle

List of castles, palaces and mansions

Entries in this list consist of: the map no. (see next pages); the name of the site; the town or area; the reference on the map; the page number in this book. Further sites are listed on page 86 – see index for complete listing.

Map of castles, palaces and mansions

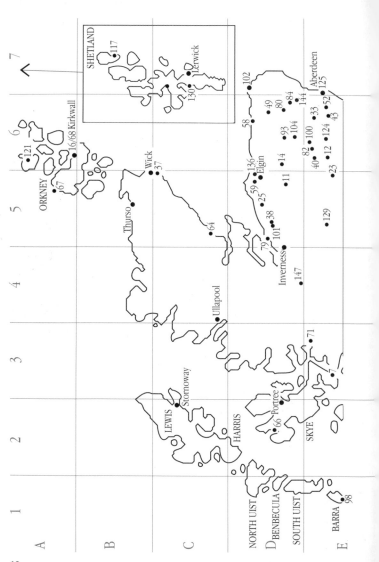

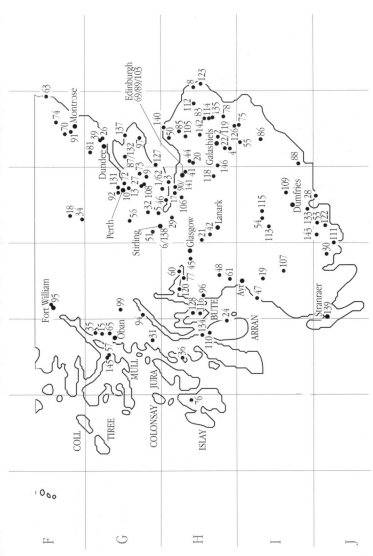

Key

P	Parking
S	Sales Area
R	Refreshments
WC	Toilet
£	Admission Charge
HS	Historic Scotland
NTS	National Trust for Scotland
Pri/LA	Private/Local Authority

Numbers before entries refer to the map on page 12-13.
Further sites are listed on page 86 – see index for full listing.
All properties are normally closed 25/26 Dec. and 1/2 Jan.
Last entrance to properties is often well before closing.

MacLellan's Castle

1 Abbot House, Dunfermline

Off A994, N of Dunfermline Abbey, Maygate, Dunfermline, Fife

Pri/LA NT 089875 65 (Ref: H5)

Abbot House dates from the 16th-century, and was built after the Reformation for the Commendator of nearby Dunfermline Abbey. Owners have included Anne of Denmark, the wife of James VI; and Lady Anne Halkett, Jacobite, herbalist and midwife. Now a heritage centre, Abbot House has displays about the house and about Dunfermline town and abbey. Garden. Dunfermline Palace and Abbey are nearby.

NOTE: [Tel: 01383 733266] Open daily all year, except closed Christmas and New Year.

P Nearby S R WC £

2 Abbotsford

On B6360, 2 miles W of Melrose, Borders.

Pri/LA NT 508343 73 (Ref: H6)

Sir Walter Scott, the famous Scottish writer and historian, bought Cartley Hole farmhouse, by the Tweed, in 1812, which he renamed Abbotsford. He had the old house demolished in 1822, and it was replaced by the main block of Abbotsford as it is today – to form a large castellated mansion with turrets, battlements and corbiestepped gables. Scott collected many historic artefacts, and there is an impressive collection of armour and weapons at the house, including Rob Roy MacGregor's gun and the Marquis of Montrose's sword. Extensive gardens and grounds. Disabled access.

NOTE: [Tel: 01896 752043] Open daily 3rd Monday in March to October.

P S R WC £

3 Aberdour Castle

On A921, Aberdour, Fife.

HS NT 193854 66 (Ref: H5)

Standing in the picturesque village of Aberdour, the large castle consists of a ruinous 14th-century keep and ranges of buildings, dating from later centuries, one of which is still roofed and contains a gallery on the first floor. A terraced garden has been restored, and there is also a fine walled garden.

Aberdour was a property of the Mortimer family. The stretch of water between the island of Inch Colm and Aberdour is known as 'Mortimer's Deep'. One of the family was a wicked fellow, but wished to be buried at the abbey on Inch Colm. His remains were on their way to the island, but were cast overboard there, either because of a storm raised from the wrath of God, or because the Abbot did not want a man such as Mortimer buried on Inch Colm.

The castle was in the possession of Thomas Randolph, a friend and captain of Robert the Bruce, in 1325; but by 1342 had passed to the Douglases. James Douglas, 4th Earl of Morton, held the castle in the 16th century. Morton was implicated in the murder of Rizzio, the secretary of Mary, Queen of Scots, and of Darnley, her second husband. He escaped severe punishment at the time, and in 1572 was made Regent for the young James VI. In 1580, however, the Earl's plotting finally caught up with him, and James VI had him executed. Much of the castle was abandoned in 1725 when the family moved to nearby Aberdour House, although part was used as a barracks, then school room, masonic hall and dwelling until 1924. Disabled access and WC.

The nearby chapel of St Fillans may date from as early as the 12th century.

NOTE: [Tel: 01383 860519]   Open daily all year except closed Thursday PM and Fridays October to March.

P S R WC £

4 Aikwood Tower

Off B7009, 4 miles W of Selkirk, Borders.

Pri/LA NT 420260 73 (Ref: H6)

Aikwood Tower is a fine rectangular 16th-century tower house. It was a property of the Scotts of Harden in the 16th century, and is said to be the birthplace of the 13th-century wizard, Sir Michael Scott of Balwearie.

Little is known of his life, but he is said to have studied at Oxford, Paris and Padua, and in Toledo in 1217. He translated works of Aristotle, and was reputedly a wizard. Aikwood is now the home of Sir David Steel, last leader of the Liberal party. Exhibition of James Hogg, the well-known Scottish writer and poet.

NOTE: [Tel: 01750 52253]   Open April to September Tuesday, Thursday and Sunday 2.00-5.00pm.

5 Alloa Tower

Off A907, in Alloa, Clackmannan.

NTS NS 889925 58 (G5)

Alloa Tower is a large 14th- or 15th-century keep with very thick walls, and still retains a fine, medieval *Alloa Tower* timber roof. The keep is crowned by a parapet with open rounds, but the building was altered in the 18th century, with the insertion of large regularly spaced windows and a new stair. A later mansion, adjoining the castle, was destroyed by fire in 1800. The tower has been renovated.

Alloa was given to Sir Robert Erskine, Great Chamberlain of Scotland, in 1360, and has remained with his descendants until the present day. Mary, Queen of Scots, was reconciled with Darnley, here in 1565; and made the family Earls of Mar. The 6th Earl 'Bobbing John' led the Jacobites in the 1715 Rising. He was so-called because he changed sides between the Hanoverians and Jacobites. The Rising was a failure, partly because of Mar's poor leadership, and he fled to France where he died, although his son recovered the lands. Although still owned by the Erskines, the tower is now in the care of the National Trust for Scotland. Collection of portraits of the Erskine family. Disabled WC and access to ground floor only.

NOTE: [Tel: 01259 211701] Open Easter weekend, then daily May to September 1.30-5.30pm.

P Nearby   S   WC   £

6 Argyll's Lodging

Off A9, Castle Wynd, Stirling.
HS   NS 793938   57   (Ref: G5)

Argyll's Lodging is a fine and well-preserved 17th-century town house. Gabled blocks with dormer windows surround a courtyard, while one side is enclosed by a wall. Many of the rooms within the lodging have recently been restored and furnished in 17th-century style.

The Lodging was built by Sir William Alexander of Menstrie, but passed to the Campbell Earls of Argyll. Archibald, 9th Earl – who was executed for treason in 1685 after leading a rising against James VII – stayed here. Exhibition. Disabled access to ground floor and WC.

NOTE: [Tel: 01786 461146] Open daily all year. Joint ticket available with Stirling Castle.

P Nearby   S   WC   £

7 Armadale Castle

Off A881, Armadale, Skye, Highlands.
Pri/LA   NG 640047   32   (Ref: E3)

Armadale Castle was built in 1815 by the architect James Gillespie Graham for the MacDonalds of Sleat, then extended in 1855 by David Bryce, although there was an earlier house here. The MacDonalds had lived at Duntulm Castle – said to have been abandoned because of the ghosts; then Monkstadt House, both on Trotternish to the north of the island: Flora MacDonald brought Bonnie Prince Charlie to Trotternish to shelter him from pursuit by Hanoverian troops in 1746. Armadale Castle, now mostly burnt out and ruinous, houses the Clan Donald centre and 'The Museum of the Isles' in some of the outbuildings. Partial disabled access and WC.

NOTE: [Tel: 01471 844305] Open daily 9.30am-5.00pm 1 April to 30 October.

P   S   R   WC   £

8 Ayton Castle

Off B9635, 2.5 miles SW of Eyemouth, Borders.
Pri/LA   NT 929614   67   (Ref: H7)

Ayton Castle, a rambling castellated mansion with a profusion of turrets, battlements and towers, stands on the site of an old castle. The old castle was besieged by the English in 1497, and held by them during the invasion of Scotland between 1547-50.

The property was held by the Aytons in medieval times, then passed to the Homes, then the

Fordyce family in 1765. In 1834 the old castle was burnt to the ground, and a new mansion, designed by James Gillespie Graham, was built in the 1840s, and then extended by the architect David Bryce in 1860. It passed to the Liddel-Grainger family, whose descendants still occupy it. Woodlands.

NOTE: [Tel: 01890 781212]   Open Sundays 10 May to 13 September or by appointment at any time.

P

9 Balgonie Castle

Off A911, 3.5 miles E of Glenrothes, Fife.

Pri/LA   NO 313007   59   (Ref: G5)

Balgonie Castle consists of a fine 14th-century keep, with a crenellated battlement and corbiestepped gables. It stands in a courtyard enclosing ranges of buildings, many of which have been restored.

The castle was built by the Sibbalds, who held the property from before 1246, but passed by marriage to Sir Robert Lundie, later Lord High Treasurer of Scotland. James IV visited the castle in 1496, as did Mary, Queen of Scots, in 1565. The property was sold in 1635 to Alexander Leslie, who fought for Gustavus Adolphus of Sweden during the 30 Years War, and was made a Field Marshal. Balgonie was captured and sacked by Rob Roy MacGregor and 200 clansmen in 1716. The castle changed hands several times, and became ruinous, but has been reoccupied and restored. Disabled access to ground floor.

The castle has many ghosts including a 'Green Lady', recorded in 1842 as being a well-known phantom; a 17th-century soldier; a dog; and in the hall apparitions and ghostly voices have been witnessed.

NOTE: [Tel: 01592 750119]   Open daily 10.00am-5.00pm all year.

P WC £

10 Balhousie Castle

Off A912, North Inch, Perth.

Pri/LA   NO 115244   58   (Ref: G5)

Balhousie Castle, a large castellated mansion of 1860 designed by David Smart, incorporates a 16th-century L-plan tower house. It was held by the Eviot family until 1478, when it was sold to the Mercers, and passed in 1625 to the Hay Earls of Kinnoul. It was taken over by the army after World War II, and in 1962 became the regimental headquarters and museum of the Black Watch. The museum features pictures, medals, uniforms and other military mementoes, telling the story of the Black Watch from its founding in 1739 to the present day.

NOTE: [Tel: 01738 621281]   Open May to September Monday to Saturday; October to April Monday to Friday (closed Christmas and New Year); closed last Saturday of June.

P S

11 Ballindalloch Castle

Off B9008, 7.5 miles SW of Charlestown of Aberlour, Moray.

Pri/LA   NJ 178365   28   (Ref: D5)

Ballindalloch Castle consists of an impressive 16th-century Z-plan tower house, which was altered and extended by ranges and wings in later centuries to form a sprawling mansion. The lands had passed to the Grants by 1499, but the castle was captured and sacked by the Gordons during a feud, and burned by the Marquis of Montrose after the Battle of Inverlochy in 1645.

In the 18th century Ballindalloch passed by marriage to the Macphersons, and is still occupied by the Macpherson-Grants. Many rooms. Gardens and grounds. Collection of 17th-century Spanish paintings. Famous breed of Aberdeen Angus cattle. Disabled access to ground floor and grounds, WC.

The castle is said to be haunted by a 'Green Lady', who has reputedly been witnessed in the dining room; as well as the ghost of General James Grant, who died in 1806.

NOTE: [Tel: 01807 500206]   Open 10.00am-5.00pm Easter to end September.

P S R WC £

12 Balmoral Castle

Off A93, 7 miles W of Ballater, Kincardine & Deeside.
Pri/LA NO 255952 44 (Ref: E6)
Balmoral Castle is a large castellated mansion, dominated by a tall turreted and battlemented tower, and was built for Prince Albert, consort of Queen Victoria, in 1855. The castle became their holiday home, and it is still often used by the royal family.

Robert II had a hunting seat here, but by 1390 a stone castle had been built. The lands were held by the Gordon family, but passed to the Farquharsons of Inverey in 1662. In 1852 Prince Albert bought the estate, and in 1855 had the present mansion built, demolishing the remains of the old castle. Disabled access to house and grounds. WC.

NOTE: [Tel: 01339 742334]   Gardens, grounds and exhibitions open to the public 10 April to 30 May daily except Sunday; 1 June to 2 August open daily.

P S R WC £

13 Balvaird Castle

Off A912, 4 miles S of Bridge of Earn, Perth & Kinross.

HS NO 169118 58 (Ref: G5)

Balvaird Castle is a fine L-plan tower house, incorporating work from the 15th century, with the remains of outbuildings in a courtyard. Balvaird was a Barclay property, but passed by marriage to the Murrays of Tullibardine in 1500, who built the castle. The family were made Viscounts Stormont and Earls of Mansfield, and they moved to Scone Palace. The castle is still owned by the Murrays, but in now in the care of the State.

NOTE: [Tel: 01786 450000]   Limited opening – confirm by phoning; other times view from exterior.

P

14 Balvenie Castle

Off A941, Dufftown, Moray.

HS NJ 326409 28 (Ref: D6)

In a pleasant location, Balvenie Castle is a large ruinous courtyard castle. It consists of a 13th-century curtain wall and deep ditch, a 16th-century L-plan tower house at one corner, and other 15th-century ranges within the courtyard. The original yett still protects the entrance.

  The Comyns built the first castle, then called Mortlach, which was destroyed or much reduced

by the forces of Robert the Bruce in 1308. Balvenie passed to the Douglases, then to John Stewart, Earl of Atholl, in 1455. Mary, Queen of Scots, visited in 1562. The castle was used by the Marquis of Montrose during his campaign of 1644-5 against the Covenanters, and it was nearby that a Covenanter force, led by Alexander Leslie, defeated a Royalist army in 1649, taking 900 prisoners. The castle was abandoned in 1724, and the ruins were put into the care of the State in 1929. Disabled WC. There are two distilleries nearby.

NOTE: [Tel: 01340 820121]   Open April to September.

P S WC £

15 Barcaldine Castle

Off A828, 4 miles N of Connel, Argyll.
Pri/LA   NM 907405   49   (Ref: G2)

Barcaldine Castle, a fine 16th-century L-plan tower house with turrets and white-washed walls, was completed by Sir Duncan Campbell of Glenorchy in 1609, and is still held by the Campbells.

The Barcaldine family were involved in the murder of Sir Colin Campbell of Glenure, the Red Fox, in 1752 which features in Robert Louis Stevenson's *Kidnapped*. John Campbell of Barcaldine, half brother of the Red Fox, tried James Stewart for the murder and had him hanged – 12 of the 15 jurors were Campbells. The castle was abandoned and became ruinous, when the family moved to nearby Barcaldine House in 1735, but it was bought back and restored from 1896.

A phantom of Harriet Campbell, a 'Blue Lady', has reputedly been seen here, and it is said that a ghostly piano can be heard on windy nights.

NOTE: [Tel: 01631 720598]   Open May to September.

P   S   R   WC   £

16 Bishop's Palace, Kirkwall

On A960, W of Kirkwall, Orkney.
HS   HY 449108   6   (Ref: A6)

The Bishop's Palace, incorporating work from the 12th century, consists of a rectangular block with a taller round tower at one end. The palace was the residence of the Bishops of Orkney from the 12th century, when Orkney was held by the Norsemen, but was rebuilt by Bishop Reid in 1541-8. King Haakon Haakonson of Norway died here in 1263 after defeat by the Scots at the Battle of Largs.

The fine and complete medieval cathedral is nearby. Also see Earl's Palace, Kirkwall.

NOTE: [Tel: 01856 875461]   Open April to September.

P Nearby   S   £

17 Blackness Castle

Off B903 or B9109, 4 miles E of Bo'ness, Falkirk.
HS   NT 056803   65   (H5)

Blackness Castle, built on a promontory in the Firth of Forth, is a grim and impressive courtyard castle. The oldest part is the tall central 15th-century keep, but the stronghold was greatly altered and strengthened for artillery in later centuries.

In medieval times Blackness was an important port for the royal burgh of Linlithgow. The castle is first mentioned in 1449 as a prison, was probably built by the Crichtons, but was burned by an English fleet in 1481. From 1537, under Sir James Hamilton of Finnart – builder of Craignethan Castle – work began to turn the castle into an artillery fort, making it one of the most formidable fortresses in Scotland at that time. Cardinal Beaton was imprisoned here in 1543. When Mary, Queen of Scots, fled to England in 1568 after the Battle of Langside, the castle held out for her until 1573.

The castle was captured by General Monck in 1650 during Cromwell's invasion of Scotland, being bombarded by land and sea, but most damage was done by a battery placed on the high ground on the landward side. It was not repaired until 1660.

In the 19th century Blackness was greatly altered to hold powder and stores, and became the central ammunition depot for Scotland. In 1912 the castle was handed over to the care of the State, and although briefly reused during World War I, a major programme of restoration and repair was carried out between 1926 and 1935. Part of *Hamlet*, starring Mel Gibson, was filmed

here, as well as the BBC production of *Ivanhoe*.
NOTE: [Tel: 01506 834807] Open daily all year, except closed Thursday PM and Fridays October to March.

P S WC £

18 Blair Castle

Off A9, 1 mile NW of Blair Atholl, Perth & Kinross.
Pri/LA NN 867662 43 (Ref: F5)
White-washed and castellated, Blair Castle is a rambling mansion of the Dukes of Atholl, and incorporates the 13th-century Comyn's Tower. The building had been completely altered and lowered in the 18th century, to turn it into a plain mansion, but was remodelled and

Blackness Castle

recastellated in 1872 by the architect David Bryce.

In 1263 the Comyns held the castle, and Edward III of England stayed here in 1336. James V visited in 1529, as did Mary, Queen of Scots, in 1564, by which time it had passed to the Earls of Atholl. In 1653 the castle was besieged, captured and partly destroyed with gunpowder by Cromwell. The castle was sufficiently complete, however, to be garrisoned by 'Bonnie Dundee', John Claverhouse, in 1689, and it was here that his body was brought after the Battle of Killiecrankie. The Earls of Atholl were made Marquises, then Dukes of Atholl in 1703.

Bonnie Prince Charlie stayed here in 1745. The following year the castle was held by Hanoverian forces, and attacked and damaged by Lord George Murray, Bonnie Prince Charlie's general and the Duke of Atholl's brother, although he failed to capture it. Blair was the last castle in Britain to be besieged.

Many interesting rooms. Collections of paintings, tapestries, arms, armour, china, costumes and Jacobite mementoes. Fine Georgian plasterwork. Garden. Disabled facilities.
NOTE: [Tel: 01796 481207] Open daily 10.00am-6.00pm 1 April to 30 October.

P S R WC £

19 Blairquhan

Off B7045, 5 miles SE of Maybole, Ayrshire.
Pri/LA NS 367055 70 (Ref: I4)

Blairquhan, a large castellated mansion designed by William Burn in 1821-4, replaced a courtyard house incorporating the 14th-century McWhurter's Tower and a range from 1573. There is a walled garden.

It was a property of the MacWhurters, but passed to the Kennedys, then the Whitefoords in 1623, then the Hunters in 1790, and is still held by the same family. Collection of furniture and pictures, including Scottish Colourists. Partial disabled access and WC.

NOTE: [Tel: 01655 770239]   Open daily 2.00-4.45pm 18 July to 16 August, except closed Mondays.

P S R WC £

20 Borthwick Castle

Off A7, 2 miles SE of
Gorebridge, Midlothian.
Pri/LA NT 370597 66 (H6)

One of the most impressive castles in Scotland, Borthwick Castle is a magnificent U-plan keep with projecting wings, separated by a deep narrow recess. The walls are massively thick; and the hall is a particularly fine room.

The castle was built by Sir William Borthwick in 1430. James Hepburn, Earl of Bothwell, and Mary, Queen of Scots, visited the castle in 1567 after their marriage and were besieged here, Mary only escaping disguised as a man. Cromwell attacked the castle in 1650, but it only took a few cannon balls for it to surrender.

NOTE: [Tel: 01875 820514]   Hotel – open mid-March to January 2 and to non-residents.

P R WC

21 Bothwell Castle

Off B7071 at Uddingston, 3 miles NW of Hamilton, Lanarkshire.
HS NS 688594 64 (Ref: H5)

Bothwell Castle is one of the largest and most impressive early stone castles in Scotland. A once magnificent round keep stands within a walled courtyard, which rises to 60 feet and encloses the remains of other buildings. The round keep, protected by a ditch, was partly dismantled in the 14th century, but is of particularly fine workmanship.

Due to its position, size and strength, Bothwell Castle was of major importance during the

Wars of Independence. It was held by the English in 1298-9, but was besieged by Scots and eventually taken after 14 months. In 1301 Edward I recaptured the castle, and it became the headquarters of the English administration. It was surrendered to the Scots in 1314 after the Battle of Bannockburn, and the keep was partly demolished at this time. In 1336 the castle was taken and rebuilt by the English, and Edward III made Bothwell his headquarters, but it was demolished again after recapture by the Scots around 1337.

The castle was rebuilt by the Earls of Douglas in the 1360s, but was partly dismantled for materials in the 17th century, and in 1935 placed in the care of the State. Exhibition.

NOTE: [Tel: 01698 816894]   Open daily all year, except closed Thursday PM and Fridays October to March.

P S WC £

22 Bowhill

Off A708, 3 miles W of Selkirk, Borders.
Pri/LA NT 426278 73 (Ref: H6)
Home of the Duke and Duchess of Buccleuch, Bowhill is an extensive rambling mansion, dating mainly from 1812, although part may date from 1708. The house was remodelled in 1831-2 by the architect William Burn. Fine collections of paintings and artefacts, including the Duke of Monmouth's saddle and execution shirt. Audio-visual presentation. Restored Victorian kitchen. Garden and country park. Disabled facilities. Ruins of Newark Castle in grounds.

NOTE: [Tel: 01750 22204]   Park open 25 April to 31 August, except closed Fridays apart from July; house open July 1.00-4.30pm.

P S R WC £

23 Braemar Castle

On A93, 0.5 miles NE of Braemar, Kincardine & Deeside.
Pri/LA NO 156924 43 (Ref: E5)
Braemar Castle is an altered 17th-century L-plan tower house, with battlemented turrets crowning the corners, and is surrounded by 18th-century star-shaped artillery defences. There is a pit-prison.

The castle was built in 1628 by John Erskine, 2nd Earl of Mar. It was captured and torched by Jacobites under Farquharson of Inverey in 1689, although it had held out against John Graham of Claverhouse. 'Bobbing John', the 6th Earl

of Mar, led the 1715 Jacobite Rising, but after its failure fled to France. The castle passed to the Farquharsons; but in 1748 was leased by the government, and turned into a barracks, the work being supervised by John Adam. The Farquharsons reoccupied the castle in the early 19th century.

The castle is said to be haunted by a blonde-haired apparition of a young woman, reputedly the ghost of a newly married bride who committed suicide, wrongly believing herself abandoned by her husband. Another ghost is reportedly that of John Farquharson of Inverey, also known as the 'Black Colonel'. Many interesting rooms.

NOTE: [Tel: 01339 741219] Open daily 10.00am-6.00pm Easter to end October, except closed Friday.

P Nearby S WC £

24 Brodick Castle

Off A841, 2 miles N of Brodick, Arran.
NTS NS 016380 69 (Ref: H3)

Brodick Castle incorporates a 15th-century keep, the lower part of which may date from the 13th century, which was extended and remodelled in the 1550s and 1650s. Extensive castellated additions were made in 1844 by the architect James Gillespie Graham.

The Stewarts built the original castle, but it was held by the English during the Wars of Independence, until 1307 when recaptured by the Scots. In 1503 it passed to the Hamilton Earls of Arran, and part was built by the 2nd Earl of Arran, who was Mary, Queen of Scots, Regent and guardian. In the 1650s the castle was occupied by Cromwell's troops.

Brodick was taken over by The National Trust for Scotland in 1958. Collections of furniture, porcelain, pictures and silver. Gardens and country park. Disabled WC and access.

A 'Grey Lady' is said to haunt the older part of the castle, her spirit possibly that of one of three women starved to death in the dungeons because they had plague.

NOTE: [Tel: 01770 302202] Open 11.30am-4.30pm daily 1 April or Good Friday (whichever sooner) to October. Garden and country park open all year.

P S R WC £

25 Brodie Castle

Off A96, 4 miles W of Forres, Moray.

NTS   NH 980578   27   (Ref: D5)

A large and impressive building, Brodie Castle consists of a massive 16th-century Z-plan tower house, with extensive additions, which was further enlarged in the 19th century by the architect William Burn.

The property was owned by the Brodies from 1160. It was burnt in 1645 because the Brodies were Covenanters, although much of the internal work survived; it was damaged by fire again

in 1786. The house was renovated in 1980 after passing to The National Trust for Scotland, although it is still occupied by the Brodies. Collection of paintings and furniture. Garden. Disabled facilities.

NOTE: [Tel: 01309 641371]   Open daily 1 April or Good Friday (whichever sooner) to September; weekends in October. Grounds open all year.

P S R WC £

26 Broughty Castle

Off A930, S of Broughty Ferry, Angus.

Pri/LA   NO 465304   54   (Ref: G6)

Standing by the sea, Broughty Castle is a tall 15th-century keep, with a later wing and artillery emplacements.

The Grays of Fowlis built the original castle in the 1490s. Patrick, 4th Lord Gray, a treacherous fellow, delivered up Broughty Castle to the English around 1547, who then raided much of the surrounding countryside. The castle was stormed by the Scots with French help in 1550, and was partly demolished. It was taken by General Monck for Cromwell in 1651, and Alexander Leslie was imprisoned here. It passed to the Fotheringham family in 1666.

Although ruinous by 1820, it was bought by the government in 1851, and restored and given gun emplacements, and was used until after World War II. The castle now houses a museum of whaling and fishery, arms and armour, and local history.

NOTE: [Tel: 01382 776121]   Open Monday-Thursdays and Saturday all year; open Sunday 2.00-5.00pm in summer; closed Friday all year; closed 1.00-2.00pm all days.

P   S

27 Burleigh Castle

On A911, 1.5 miles N of Kinross, Perth & Kinross.

HS   NO 130046   58   (Ref: G5)

Although once a large and imposing castle, Burleigh Castle now consists of a ruined 15th-century keep, a section of courtyard wall with a gate, and a corner tower. It was a property of the Balfours of Burleigh, and visited by James IV. In 1707 the Master of Burleigh fell in love with a young servant girl, and was sent abroad to forget her. He swore if she married he would return and slay her husband. She married Henry Stenhouse, the schoolmaster of Inverkeithing, and Burleigh duly returned then shot and killed the poor man. In 1709 Burleigh was captured, tried and sentenced to be beheaded. He managed to escape by exchanging clothes with his sister, and fled to the continent. He returned and fought for the Jacobites in the 1715 Rising, after which the family were forfeited. Burleigh died unmarried in 1757.

NOTE: Open all year.

P Nearby

28 Caerlaverock Castle

Off B725, 7 miles SE of Dumfries.

HS   NY 026656   84   (Ref: J5)

Once a formidable fortress and still a magnificent ruin, Caerlaverock Castle consists of a triangular courtyard with a gatehouse at one side, round towers at two corners, and ranges of buildings between, all still surrounded by a wet moat.

The castle was built in the 13th century by the Maxwells, but was captured by Edward I of England in 1300, although it was eventually recaptured by the Scots. Murdoch Stewart, son of Robert Duke of Albany, was imprisoned in the castle before being executed in 1425. James V visited the castle prior to defeat at Solway Moss in 1542. The castle was surrendered to the English in 1545, but was later recaptured by the Scots. In 1640 Caerlaverock was taken by a force of Covenanters after a siege of 13 weeks, and

dismantled. The castle was transferred to the care of the State in 1946. Visitor centre, children's park and nature trail to old castle. Video presentation. Reasonable disabled access and WC.

NOTE: [Tel: 01387 770244]   Open daily all year.

P   S   R   WC   £

29 Callendar House

Off A803, Falkirk.

Pri/LA   NS 898794   65   (Ref: H5)

Callendar House, an large ornate mansion of the 1870s with towers and turrets, incorporates a 14th- or 15th-century castle.

It was held by the Livingstone family from 1345, who were made Earls of Callendar in 1641. Mary, Queen of Scots, stayed here several times in the 1560s. The castle was stormed and captured by Cromwell in 1650, and later used as his headquarters by General Monck. The Livingstones were forfeited for their part in the 1715 Jacobite Rising, and Bonnie Prince Charlie stayed here in 1745. Visitor centre, and restored kitchen of the 1820s. History research centre. Disabled access to all house and lift.

NOTE: [Tel: 01324 503770]   Open all year Monday to Saturday; daily July and August.

P Nearby   S   R   WC   £

30 Cardoness Castle

Off B796, 0.75 miles SW of Gatehouse of Fleet, Galloway.

HS   NX 591552   83   (Ref: J4)

Standing on a rocky mound, Cardoness Castle consists of a ruinous late 15th-century rectangular keep and a courtyard, which enclosed outbuildings.

Cardoness passed to the MacCullochs by marriage around 1450. They were an unruly lot, and the last of the family was Sir Gordon MacCulloch, who shot Gordon of Buck o'Bield in 1690, fled abroad, returned and was spotted in a church in Edinburgh. He was beheaded by the Maiden, an early Scottish guillotine preserved in the National Museum of Scotland in Edinburgh. Cardoness had passed to the Gordons in 1629, then to the Maxwells. Visitor centre.

NOTE: [Tel: 01557 814427]   Open daily April to September, but weekends only October to March.

P   S   WC   £

31 Carnasserie Castle

Off A816, 8.5 miles N of Lochgilphead, Argyll.

HS   NM 837009   55   (Ref: G3)

Carnasserie Castle consists of a ruined 16th-century tower house and lower hall-block. It was built by John Carswell, who published the first ever book in Gaelic in 1567, the Gaelic version of the Book of Common Order. He was Parson of Kilmartin, and was made the Protestant Bishop of Argyll and the Isles in 1566. On his death in 1572, Carnasserie passed to the Campbells of Auchinbreck, and it was captured and sacked in 1685 by the MacLeans and MacLachlans during Archibald Campbell, 9th Earl of Argyll's rebellion.

NOTE: Open all year.

P

32 Castle Campbell

Off A91, 0.5 miles N of Dollar, Clackmannan.

NTS   NS 962994   58   (Ref: G5)

An impressive and picturesque ruin in a wonderful location, Castle Campbell was built where the Burns of Care and Sorrow join, overlooked by Gloom Hill, and was originally known as Castle Gloom. A large strong 15th-century keep, altered in later centuries, stands at one corner

of a substantial ruinous courtyard, enclosed by a curtain wall.

It was a property of the Stewarts, but passed by marriage to Colin Campbell, 1st Earl of Argyll and Chancellor of Scotland, and he had the name changed to Castle Campbell. Cromwell's forces occupied the castle in 1653, and only part was restored after being torched by General Monck in 1654. In 1948 the castle was taken over by the National Trust for Scotland, but is administered by Historic Scotland. Garden.

The walk up from lower car park, through Dollar Glen, is closed at the time of writing, due to rock falls.

NOTE: [Tel: 01259 742408]   Open daily all year except Thursday PM and Fridays October to March. Administered by Historic Scotland.

P S R WC £

33 Castle Fraser

Off B993 or B977, 6.5 miles SW of Inverurie, Aberdeenshire.

NTS NJ 724126 38 (Ref: E6)

Magnificent and well preserved, Castle Fraser is a tall and massive Z-plan tower house, mostly dating from between 1575 and 1636. Two projecting wings form a courtyard, the final side being completed by other buildings, one with an arched gateway.

The property was acquired by the Frasers in 1454, who in 1633 were made Lords Fraser, and they built the castle. The Frasers were Covenanters, and their lands were ravaged in 1638, and again in 1644 by the Marquis of Montrose. The family were later Jacobites, and the 4th Lord died a fugitive, falling from a cliff, after the 1715 Rising. The property remained with the Frasers until 1921, but is now cared for by The National Trust for Scotland. Many interesting rooms. Walled garden. Disabled facilities.

NOTE: [Tel: 01330 833463]   Castle open Easter weekend; then daily May to September; weekends only in October. Garden open all year.

P S R WC £

34 Castle Menzies

Off B846, 1.5 miles NW of Aberfeldy, Perthshire.

Pri/LA NN 837496 52 (Ref: F5)

Castle Menzies is a fine altered and extended 16th-century tower house, consisting of a main block and two taller square towers, projecting at opposite corners. Many turrets crown the building. An extension was added by the architect William Burn in 1840.

It was a property of the Menzies family. The castle was occupied by Cromwell's force in the 1650s, and was captured by Jacobites in 1715. Bonnie Prince Charlie stayed here for two nights in 1746, but soon after the castle was seized by Hanoverian forces, led by the Duke of Cumberland, the butcher of Culloden. The Menzies family held the property until 1918, and it was purchased by the Menzies Clan Society in 1957.

Many rooms. Museum about the Menzies clan, including Bonnie Prince Charlie's death mask. Disabled access to part of ground floor, tea room and gift shop.

NOTE: [Tel: 01887 820982]   Open April or Easter to 17 October Monday to Saturday 10.30am to 5.00pm, Sunday 2.00 to 5.00pm.

P S R WC £

35 Castle Stalker

Off A828, 14 miles N of Connel, Argyll.

Pri/LA NM 921473 49 (Ref: G3)

Standing dramatically on a small island in a magnificent location, Castle Stalker is a tall, massive and simple keep. It was built by Duncan Stewart of Appin, who was made Chamberlain of the Isles. In 1620 the castle was sold to the Campbells, but the Stewarts retrieved it after a long siege in 1685; although the garrison surrendered to William and Mary's forces only five years later. In 1715 the clan fought for the Jacobites at Sheriffmuir. The 9th Chief did not support the 1745 Jacobite Rising – the clan were led by Stewart of Ardsheal – and the lands were sold in 1765. The castle was abandoned about 1780, but restored from ruin in the 1960s.

NOTE: [Tel: 01631 730234 or 01883 622768]   Open by appointment from April to September. Telephone for details (£6.00 admission charge).

P Nearby

36 Castle Sween

Off B8024, 11 miles NW of Tarbert, Argyll.

HS NR 712789 62 (Ref: H3)

Standing on a rocky ridge, Castle Sween is an impressive 11th- or 12th-century castle of enclosure, consisting of a curtain wall, enclosing a rectangular courtyard, and a strong 15th-century keep.

One of the earliest castles in Scotland, it was built at a time when this part of Scotland was still under Norse rule, and is said to be named after Sueno, an 11th-century Dane. The castle was held by the MacSweens, until captured by Robert the Bruce in 1315; then the MacMillans; the Stewarts of Menteith; then the MacNeils of Gigha for the MacDonald Lord of the Isles. In 1481 the Campbells became keepers for the Crown. The castle was captured and partly dismantled by Alaisdair Colkitto MacDonald in 1647. One tower collapsed in the 19th century, but it has since been consolidated.

NOTE: Open all year.

P Nearby

37 Castle of Old Wick

Off A9, 1 mile S of Wick, Caithness.

HS ND 369488 12 (Ref: C5)

One of the oldest castles in Scotland, Castle of Old Wick consists of a simple square keep standing on a promontory on cliffs above the sea, cut off by a ditch.

It was built in the 12th century when this part of Scotland was ruled from Orkney by the Norsemen, possibly by Harold Maddadson, Earl of Caithness, who was blinded and castrated by Alexander II. It was a property of the Cheynes in the 14th century, then the Oliphants, before passing to the Dunbars of Hempriggs, then the Sutherland Lord Duffus. In 1569, during a feud with the Sinclairs, the castle was besieged, starved into submission, and captured by John Sinclair, Master of Caithness. It was sold to the Sinclairs in 1606.

NOTE: Open all year - great care must be taken.

38 Cawdor Castle

Off B9090, 5 miles SW of Nairn, Highlands.

Pri/LA NH 847499 27 (Ref: D5)

One of the most magnificent and well-preserved strongholds in Scotland, Cawdor Castle incorporates a tall plain keep, dating from the 14th century, although the parapet and upper

works were added in 1454. The castle has a deep ditch crossed by a drawbridge, and there are gabled ranges, crowned with turrets. Defending the entrance is a massive iron yett, brought here from Lochindorb Castle after 1455.

The title 'Thane of Cawdor' is associated with Macbeth, but Duncan was not murdered here – as the castle is not nearly old enough – and anyway he died in battle near Spynie. The 5th Thane built much of the present castle, but the Campbells obtained Cawdor by in 1511 kidnapping the girl heiress, Muriel Calder, and marrying her at the age of 12 to the Earl of Argyll's son, Sir John Campbell. Campbell of Inverliver led the kidnapping, and all six of his sons were slain.

The Campbells of Cawdor, her descendants, remained at the castle, and were made Earls of Cawdor in 1827. Fine collections of portraits, furnishings and tapestries. Gardens. Three shops: gift shop, wool and book shop. Golf course. Disabled access to grounds; some of castle.

NOTE: [Tel: 01667 404615]   Open 10.00am-5.00pm daily 1 May to 12 October.

P S R WC £

39 Claypotts Castle

Off A92, 3.5 miles E of Dundee.
HS NO 452319 54 (Ref: G6)

An unusual and impressive building, Claypotts Castle is a Z-plan tower house, consisting of a rectangular main block and two large round towers, crowned with square gabled chambers, at opposite corners.

The lands passed from the Abbey of Lindores to the Strachans about 1560, and the castle was built soon afterwards. It was sold to the Grahams in 1620, one of whom was John Graham of Claverhouse, Viscount Dundee, who was known as 'Bloody Clavers' for his cruel persecution of Covenanters in Galloway; and 'Bonnie Dundee' after his death in 1689 at the victory over

the forces of William and Mary at the Battle of Killiecrankie. His lands were forfeited in 1694 and went to the Douglas Earl of Angus, then later to the Homes. In the 19th century the castle was used to house farm labourers, but is now managed by Historic Scotland.

NOTE: [Tel: 01786 450000]   Limited opening, confirm by telephone.

40 Corgarff Castle

Off A939, 10 miles NW of Ballater, Aberdeenshire.
HS NJ 255086 37 (Ref: E6)

Corgarff Castle consists of a much-altered rectangular 16th-century tower house, white-washed and restored, with later pavilions and star-shaped outworks.

The castle was built about 1530 by the Elphinstones, and leased to the Forbes family. It was torched in 1571 by Adam Gordon of Auchindoun, killing Margaret Campbell, wife of Forbes of Towie, and 26 others of her household. The Erskine Earls of Mar acquired the lands in 1626, but the castle was burnt by Jacobites in 1689; then again in 1716, this time by Hanoverians to punish the Earl of Mar for his part in the Jacobite Rising; and for a third time in 1746.

In 1748 the government bought Corgarff, remodelled the tower, and used it as a barracks after the Jacobite Risings. It was later used as a base to help stop illicit whisky distilling, but was abandoned in 1831, and placed into the care of the State in 1961. Exhibition: one of the floors houses a restored barrack room. Whisky still.

NOTE: [Tel: 01975 651460] Open daily April to September; open weekends only October to March

P S £

41 Craigmillar Castle

Off A68, 2.5 miles SE of Edinburgh Castle.

HS NT 288709 66 (Ref: H5)

A strong, imposing and well-preserved ruin, Craigmillar Castle consists of a 14th-century L-plan keep, surrounded by a 15th-century curtain wall with round corner towers. Early in the 16th century it was given an additional walled courtyard, protected by a ditch.

The Prestons held the property from 1374, and built a new castle on the site of a much older stronghold. In 1477 James III imprisoned his brother John, Earl of Mar, in one of its cellars, where he died. The Earl of Hertford burnt the castle in 1544, after valuables placed here by the citizens of Edinburgh had been stolen by the English. James V visited the castle to escape 'the pest' in Edinburgh.

Mary, Queen of Scots, used Craigmillar often, and fled here in 1566 after the murder of Rizzio by, among others, her second husband Darnley. It was also here that the Regent Moray, Bothwell and William Maitland of Lethington plotted Darnley's murder. Mary's son, James VI, also visited.

A walled-up skeleton was found in one of the vaults in 1813. The castle featured in the BBC production of *Ivanhoe*. Exhibition and visitor centre.

NOTE: [Tel: 0131 661 4445]   Open daily all year except closed Thursday PM and Fridays October to March.

P S £

42 Craignethan Castle

Off A72, 4.5 miles W of Lanark.
HS NS 816464 72 (Ref: H5)

Standing on a promontory above a deep ravine, Craignethan is an early castle built to withstand artillery. A strong tower was surrounded by a curtain wall on three sides, with a massively

thick rampart protecting the landward side. There was also an outer courtyard. Much of the castle is now ruinous, although the main tower survives.

Sir James Hamilton of Finnart, a talented architect and the King's Superintendent of Palaces, built most of the castle. Hamilton was beheaded for treason in 1540, although his son eventually inherited his lands. Mary, Queen of Scots, is said to have spent the night here before the Battle of Langside in 1568. The Hamiltons formed the main part of her army, but were defeated by the Regent Moray, and Mary fled to England. The garrison of Craignethan surrendered after the battle, but the castle was retaken by the Hamiltons, then attacked in 1579 and given up without a siege. The defences were then demolished. Craignethan passed to the Hays in 1665, and into the care of the State in 1949. Exhibition.

NOTE: [Tel: 01555 860364]   Open daily April to September; open daily March and October except Thursday PM and Friday; closed November to February.

P S R WC £

43 Crathes Castle

Off A93, 3 miles E of Banchory, Kincardine & Deeside.

NTS NO 734968 45 (Ref: E6)

One of the finest surviving castles in Scotland, Crathes Castle is a massive 16th-century tower house, square in plan. The upper storeys are adorned with much corbelling, turrets, and decoration, while the lower storeys are very plain apart from a large modern window. There is a small extension, and a large adjoining mansion has been demolished.

The property was owned by the Burnetts of Leys from the 14th century, their original castle being in the now drained Loch of Leys. The jewelled ivory 'Horn of Leys' is kept at Crathes,

and was given to the Burnetts in 1323 by Robert the Bruce. Around 1553, the family began to build the new castle at Crathes, but it was not completed until 1596. It passed to The National Trust for Scotland in 1951.

One of the chambers, the Green Lady's room, is said to be haunted. The ghost reportedly first appeared in the 18th century, and is seen crossing the chamber, with a baby in her arms, to disappear at the fireplace. The young woman seems to have been a daughter of the then laird, and had been dallying with a servant. It appears that she was murdered to hide her pregnancy. A skeleton of a baby was reportedly found by workmen under the hearthstone. The spectre is said to have been seen many times.

Many rooms, some with original painted ceilings. Collections of portraits and furniture. Grounds. Walled garden, consisting of eight separate gardens with unusual plants. Children's adventure playground. Disabled access to ground floor of castle and grounds; WC.

NOTE: [Tel: 01330 844525]   Open April to October. Grounds and garden open all year. Timed ticket arrangement for castle; garden may be closed at short notice on very busy days (limited parking).

P S R WC £

44 Crichton Castle

Off B6367, 2 miles E of Gorebridge, Midlothian.
HS NT 380612 66 (Ref: H6)

A complex, large and interesting building, Crichton Castle consists of ruinous ranges of buildings from the 14th to 16th centuries, enclosing a small courtyard. One feature is the arcaded, diamond-faced facade of a 16th-century range, decorated in the Italian Renaissance style.

The castle was a property of the Crichtons, and probably first built about 1370. Sir William Crichton, Chancellor of Scotland, entertained the young Earl of Douglas and his brother before

having them murdered in 1440 at the 'Black Dinner' in Edinburgh Castle. John Forrester slighted the castle in retaliation.

The Crichtons were forfeited for treason in 1488, and the property later passed to Patrick Hepburn, Lord Hailes, who was made Earl of Bothwell. Mary, Queen of Scots, attended a wedding here in 1562. Crichton passed through the hands of many families, was abandoned, and became a romantic ruin. It was put into the care of the State in 1926.

NOTE: [Tel: 01875 320017]   Open April to September – walk to property.

P S £

45 Crookston Castle

Off A736, 3 miles E of Paisley.
NTS NS 524628 64 (Ref: H4)

Surrounded by a large ditch – now in the middle of a housing estate – Crookston Castle is an unusual ruined irregularly-shaped 13th-century keep. The keep is strengthened by towers at the corners, only one of which is fairly intact, formerly making it X-plan.

The lands passed by marriage in the 13th century to the Stewart Earls of Lennox. During the rebellion of the Earl of Lennox in the 15th century, James IV bombarded the castle with the large cannon, 'Mons Meg' – which is kept at Edinburgh Castle – leading to a quick surrender. Mary, Queen of Scot's husband, Henry Stewart, Lord Darnley, owned it; and they may have been betrothed here, rather than at Wemyss Castle, or have stayed here after their marriage. It passed through many families, including the Graham Dukes of Montrose, who in 1757 sold it to the Maxwells of Pollok. The castle became ruinous, but was partly restored in 1847 to commemorate Queen Victoria's first visit to Glasgow. It was gifted to The National Trust for Scotland in 1931, their first property.

NOTE: [Tel: 0141 332 7133] Open all year – key available from Castle Cottage at reasonable times. Administered by Historic Scotland.

P Nearby

46 Culross Palace

Off B9037, Culross, Fife.

NTS NS 986862 65 (Ref: H5)

Set in the picturesque village of Culross, the Palace, built between 1597 and 1611, consists of yellow-washed ranges of gabled buildings, with decorative paint work and original interiors.

There is an unusual steeply terraced garden. The Palace was built for Sir George Bruce of Carnock, who made a fortune in coal mining, but about 1700 passed to the Erskines. The building has been carefully restored by the National Trust for Scotland. Disabled access to exhibition. Town House and Study.

NOTE: [Tel: 01383 880359] Open April to September.

P Nearby S R WC £

47 Culzean Castle

Off A77, 4.5 miles W of Maybole, Ayrshire.

NTS NS 233103 70 (Ref: I4)

Pronounced 'Cul-lane', Culzean Castle is a magnificent sprawling castellated mansion built between 1777-92. The present building incorporates part of the original castle, which itself was built on the site of an older stronghold.

Culzean was a property of the Kennedys from the 12th century. Thomas Kennedy of Culzean was murdered by the Mure Lord Auchendrane in the course of a feud. The castle was completely rebuilt for the 9th and 10th Earls of Cassillis by the architect Robert Adam. In 1945 it passed to The National Trust for Scotland. A flat within the building was reserved for use by President Dwight Eisenhower for his services to Britain during World War II.

Fine interiors. Collections of paintings and furniture. Country park and visitor centre – one of the foremost attractions in Scotland.

NOTE: [Tel: 01655 760274] Open April to October. Park open all year.

P S R WC £

48 Dean Castle

Off B7038, 1 mile NE of Kilmarnock, Ayrshire.
Pri/LA NS 437394 70 (Ref: H4)

Interesting and well preserved, Dean Castle consists of a 14th-century keep and a 15th-century palace block within a courtyard, all enclosed by a curtain wall.

The lands were given to the Boyds by Robert the Bruce, and a castle here is said to have been besieged by the English during the Wars of Independence. Robert Boyd became Guardian of James III during his minority, and practically ruled Scotland from 1466-9. He later had to flee to Denmark, and his brother was executed for treason. William, 10th Lord Boyd, was created Earl of Kilmarnock in 1661.

The 4th Earl was Privy Councillor to Bonnie Prince Charlie during the Jacobite Rising of 1745. He was a Colonel in the Prince's guard, but was captured after the Battle of Culloden in 1746 and executed by beheading, his lands and titles forfeited.

In 1735 a fire had gutted the hall block, and most of the castle was abandoned. It was restored from 1905, and the castle now houses a museum, containing a collection of armour and musical instruments, and is surrounded by a public park.

NOTE: [Tel: 01563 574916] Open daily April to end October from 12.00-5.00pm; open end October to end March weekends only; closed Christmas and New Year.

P S R WC £

49 Delgatie Castle

Off A947, 2 miles E of Delgatie, Banff & Buchan.
Pri/LA NJ 755506 29 (Ref: D6)

An imposing and original building, Delgatie Castle consists of a 15th-century keep, an adjoining 16th-century gabled house, and lower later buildings, although it said to incorporate work from the 11th century.

Delgatie was originally held by the Comyn Earls of Buchan, but passed to the Hays in the 14th century, who were created Earls of Errol in 1452. Sir Gilbert Hay of Delgatie, with many others of the family, was killed at the Battle of Flodden in 1513. Mary, Queen of Scots, spent three days here in 1562. The 9th Earl was summoned for treason in 1594 for supporting the Gordon Earl of Huntly, and part of the west wall was battered down by James VI's forces. Sir William Hay of Delgatie was standard bearer to the Marquis of Montrose, during his campaign of 1645. Although defeated at Philiphaugh, Hay managed to return the standard to Buchanan Castle, but he was executed with Montrose at Edinburgh in 1650, and buried beside him in St Giles Cathedral. The Hays supported the Jacobites during the 1715 and 1745 Risings, and the castle passed from the family, although they eventually recovered it. Delgatie was made the Clan Hay centre in 1948.

NOTE: [Tel: 01888 563479] Open daily April to October 10.00am-5.00pm.

P S R WC £

50 Dirleton Castle

Off A198, 2 miles W of North Berwick, East Lothian.

NTS NT 518840 66 (Ref: H6)

Standing on a rock, Dirleton Castle consists of ruinous towers and ranges of buildings around a courtyard, which were once surrounded by a wide ditch. The old part of the castle, dating from the 13th century, is grouped around a small triangular court, and consists of a large

drum tower, a smaller round tower and a rectangular tower.

  The castle was built in the 13th century by the De Vaux family. It was captured after a hard siege in 1298, when the English employed large engines, but was retaken by the Scots in 1311 and partly demolished. In the 15th century the castle passed to the Halyburton family, who extended it; and in the 16th century to the Ruthvens, who again remodelled much of the castle; then in 1600 to the Erskines of Gogar.

  In 1650 the castle was besieged by General Monck, during Cromwell's invasion of Scotland, and quickly forced to surrender. The castle was abandoned soon afterwards, and became ruinous. Fine gardens. Exhibition.

NOTE: [Tel: 01620 850330] Open daily all year. Administered by Historic Scotland.

S £

51 Doune Castle

Off A820, SE of Doune, Stirlingshire.

HS NN 728011 57 (Ref: G5)

Standing on a strong site in a lovely location, Doune Castle, built in the 14th century, consists of two strong towers linked by a lower range. These buildings form two sides of a courtyard, the other sides enclosed by a high curtain wall. The fine Lord's Hall has a carved oak screen, musician's gallery and a double fireplace.

  The castle was built by Robert Stewart, Duke of Albany, who virtually ruled Scotland during the reign of Robert III and the imprisonment in England of the young James I. When Albany died in 1420, his son, Murdoch, succeeded him as Regent, but when James I was freed in 1424 he had Murdoch executed.

Doune was kept as a royal hunting lodge, prison, and dower house for the widows of James III, James IV and James V. It was occasionally used by Mary, Queen of Scots, and was held by forces loyal to her until 1570. Doune was occupied by the Marquis of Montrose in 1645, and by Government troops during the Jacobite Risings of 1689 and 1715. It was taken by Jacobites in 1745, and used as a prison, although many of the prisoners escaped. Doune was restored in the late 19th century, and was used as a location for the BBC production of *Ivanhoe*. Exhibition.

NOTE: [Tel: 01786 841742]   Open daily all year except closed Thursday PM and Fridays October to March.

P S £

52 Drum Castle

Off A93, 3 miles W of Peterculter, Kincardine & Deeside.
NTS NJ 796005 38 (Ref: E6)

One of the oldest occupied houses in Scotland and surrounded by extensive gardens, Drum Castle consists of a plain 13th-century keep of four storeys. To this has been added a large L-shaped range of 1619, and the castle was extended again in the 19th century.

Drum was a property of the Irvines from 1323, when the lands were given to them by Robert the Bruce after Sir William de Irwyn, or Irvine, whose seat was at Bonshaw, had been his standard bearer. Sir Alexander Irvine was killed at the Battle of Harlaw in 1411, slain by and slaying MacLean of Duart 'Hector of the Battles'. The Irvines supported Charles I, and Drum was besieged and plundered by Argyll in 1644, and sacked again in 1645 when the womenfolk were turned out of the castle. The family were Jacobites and fought in the 1715 and 1745 Jacobite Risings.

The courtyard was remodelled by David Bryce in 1876. In 1975 the castle was given to The

National Trust for Scotland. Collections of furniture and pictures. Garden. Disabled facilities.
NOTE: [Tel: 01330 811204]   Castle open Easter weekend; May to September; weekends only in October. Garden as house. Grounds open all year.

P S R WC £

53 Drumcoltran Tower
Off A711, 5 miles NE of Dalbeattie, Galloway.
HS NX 869683 84 (Ref: J5)
Located in the middle of a farm, Drumcoltran Castle is a 16th-century L-plan tower house, which was built by the Maxwells. It was sold to the Irvings in 1669, then to the Hynds in 1799, then the Herons, and then the Maxwells in 1875. The tower was occupied until the 1890s.
NOTE: Open all year.

P Nearby

54 Drumlanrig Castle
Off A76, 3 miles NW of Thornhill, Dumfriesshire.
Pri/LA NX 851992 78 (Ref: I5)
Drumlanrig is an impressive 17th-century courtyard mansion, consisting of four ranges around a courtyard, with higher rectangular towers at the corners. The towers have pepperpot turrets. The remains of a 14th-century castle, including cellars, were built into the mansion.

  The original castle was built by the Douglases soon after 1357, but was sacked by the English in 1549. It was destroyed in 1575 because the family supported Mary, Queen of Scots, who had stayed here in 1563. However, it was restored or rebuilt as James VI stayed here in 1617, and Drumlanrig was occupied by a Cromwellian force in 1650.

  A huge new mansion, set around the courtyard, was built between 1675 and 1689 by the architect William Wallace for William Douglas, 3rd Earl of Queensberry, who was made Duke in 1684. It passed to the Scott Dukes of Buccleuch in 1810. There is a fine collection of pictures, including paintings by Rembrandt, Holbein and Leonardo, as well as many other works of art. Gardens. Visitor centre.
NOTE: [Tel: 01848 330248]   Open daily 2 May to 23 August 12.00-4.00pm.

P S R WC £

55 Drumlanrig's Tower
Off A7, in Hawick, Borders.
Pri/LA NT 502144 79 (Ref: I6)
Drumlanrig's Tower consists of an altered and extended 16th-century L-plan tower house, once surrounded by a moat. It was a property of the Douglases of Drumlanrig, and the only building left unburnt after the torching of Hawick by the English in 1570. It was later occupied by Anna, Duchess of Buccleuch, wife of the executed Duke of Monmouth. From the 17th century, part of the basement was used as prison, this becoming the wine-cellar on its conversion to a coaching inn. The hotel was closed in 1970, and the tower was restored to house an exhibition, with 10 galleries covering 800 years of Border history.
NOTE: [Tel: 01450 373457]   Open daily March to October.

P Nearby S £

56 Drummond Castle

Off A822, 2.5 miles SW of Crieff, Perthshire.
Pri/LA NN 844181 58 (Ref: G5)

Built on a rocky outcrop, Drummond Castle consists of a 15th-century keep to which has been added a lower 17th-century extension, and a late 19th-century mansion, which was remodelled from the buildings surrounding the keep.

Sir Malcolm Drummond distinguished himself at the Battle of Bannockburn in 1314, and was given the lands here – although the existing castle was not begun until the 15th century.

Margaret Drummond, daughter of the builder, was a lover of James IV, and they were reputedly married and had a daughter. However, some of the nobles wanted James to marry Margaret Tudor, sister of Henry VIII of England. To this end, and to 'free' James, Margaret, and two of her sisters, were murdered with poisoned sugared fruit, and are buried side by side in Dunblane Cathedral.

The Drummonds were made Earls of Perth. Mary, Queen of Scots, visited the castle in 1566-7 with Bothwell. The castle was badly damaged by Cromwell in the 1650s, and slighted after having been occupied by Hanoverian troops during the Jacobite Rising of 1715. The 5th Earl had commanded the Jacobite cavalry at the Battle of Sheriffmuir that year, and the 6th commanded the left wing of the Jacobite army at the Battle of Culloden in 1746. The family was forfeited as a result, and the castle passed from the family. The Earldom of Perth was recovered in 1853, but they now live at Stobhall. The castle and magnificent formal garden featured in the film version of *Rob Roy.*

NOTE: [Tel: 01764 681257]   Castle not open. Gardens open Easter weekend and then daily May to October 2.00-5.00pm.

P S WC £

57 Duart Castle

Off A849, 3 miles S of Craignure, Mull.
Pri/LA NM 749354 49 (Ref: G3)

An extremely impressive and daunting fortress, Duart Castle consists of a large 13th-century curtain wall, enclosing a courtyard on a rocky knoll. In 1390 Lachlan Lubanach, 5th Chief, built

the keep on the outside of the curtain wall, enclosing the existing well. There are later ranges of buildings within the walls.

The MacLeans of Duart claim descent from Gillean of the Battle Axe. Lachlan Lubanach married Lady Elizabeth, daughter of the Lord of the Isles, granddaughter of Robert II King of Scots, and was granted the first known charter for Duart dated 1390 as her dowry. While fighting with the MacDonalds, the 6th chief Red Hector was killed at the Battle of Harlaw in 1411, slaying and being slain by Sir Alexander Irvine of Drum.

Lachlan Cattanach, 11th Chief, became so unhappy with his Campbell wife that he had the poor woman chained to a rock in the Firth of Lorn to be drowned at high tide. However, she was rescued and taken to her father, the Campbell Earl of Argyll. As a result, MacLean was murdered in his bed at Edinburgh by Sir John Campbell of Cawdor.

In 1674 the castle was acquired by the Campbell Earl of Argyll. The MacLeans remained staunch Jacobites throughout Risings. Although garrisoned, the castle was not used as a residence, and was abandoned after the Rising of 1745 to become derelict and roofless. It was acquired in 1911 by Fitzroy MacLean, who restored the castle. It houses a display of clan memorabilia. Tea room and shop located in converted byre directly below the castle.

NOTE: [Tel: 01680 812309]   Open May to mid-October daily 10.30-6.00pm.

P S R WC £

58 Duff House

Off A97, Banff.

HS NJ 692633   29   (Ref: D6)

Duff House, a fine mansion with colonnades and corner towers, dates from 1735, and was designed by William Adam for William Duff of Braco, later Earl of Fife. The house is now used to display works of art from the National Galleries of Scotland. Disabled facilities including lift and WC.

NOTE: [Tel: 01261 818181]   Open daily all year except closed Tuesday April to September and closed Monday-Wednesday October to March.

P S R WC £

59 Duffus Castle

Off B9012 or B9135, 3 miles NW of Elgin, Moray.

HS NJ 189672   28   (Ref: D5)

One of the best examples of a 12th-century motte and bailey castle in Scotland, Duffus Castle consists of an extensive outer bailey with a wet moat, a walled and ditched inner bailey, and a large motte. On the motte was built a square 14th-century stone keep, part of which has collapsed down the slope.

The original castle was built by Freskin, Lord of Strathbrock. David I stayed here while supervising the construction of nearby Kinloss Abbey. Duffus was destroyed by the Scots in 1297, but was rebuilt in stone by the Cheynes in the 14th century. It passed by marriage to the Sutherland Lord Duffus in 1350, and the family held the property until 1843. The castle was sacked in 1452 by the Douglas Earl of Moray, and again in 1645 by Royalists. John Graham of Claverhouse, 'Bonnie' Dundee' stayed here in 1689. The castle was abandoned for nearby Duffus House, at the end of the 17th century, and became ruinous.

NOTE: Open all year.

P

60 Dumbarton Castle

Off A814, in Dumbarton.

HS NS 400745 64 (Ref: H4)

Standing on a commanding rock on the north shore of the Clyde, little remains of the medieval Dumbarton Castle, which now consists of 18th and 19th century fortifications, except the 14th-century entrance.

Meaning 'fortress of the Britons', Dumbarton is first mentioned around 450 as the stronghold of the kings of Strathclyde. In 756 it was captured by Picts and Northumbrians, and in 870 was besieged by Irish raiders, who captured the rock only after four months of fighting, starving the garrison into surrender. Owen the Bald, the last King of Strathclyde, died at the Battle of Carham in 1018, and Strathclyde was absorbed into the kingdom of Scots.

Dumbarton became a royal castle, and was a formidable fortress. William Wallace was held here before being taken to London for execution in 1305. In 1333 the young David II sheltered in the castle during fighting with the English. James IV besieged Dumbarton twice in 1489 to remove the Earl of Lennox, the second time successfully, and then used it as a base to destroy the Lord of the Isles. After the disastrous Battle of Pinkie in 1547, the infant Mary, Queen of Scots, was kept at Dumbarton for some months before being taken to France. The Earl of Morton and Patrick Stewart, 3rd Earl of Orkney, were imprisoned here before execution in 1581 and 1614 respectively. In 1654 a Royalist force made a successful surprise attack on Cromwell's garrison.

The castle was badly damaged during this period, and was then developed for artillery over the coming centuries. Exhibition in Governor's House.

NOTE: [Tel: 01389 732167] Open daily all year except closed Thursday PM and Fridays October to March.

P S WC £

61 Dundonald Castle

Off B730, 3.5 miles NE of Troon, Ayrshire.

HS NS 364345 70 (Ref: H4)

Dundonald Castle consists of a remodelled 13th-century keep, formerly the gatehouse of an earlier castle, which is said to have been slighted in the Wars of Independence. The entrance was blocked, and the basement and hall on the first floor were given vaults, the hall vault being particularly fine. Most of the wall of the adjoining courtyard survives.

Dundonald was built by the Stewarts in the 13th century, and was extended and remodelled around 1350 by Robert II, who died at Dundonald in 1390. Robert III also used the castle, and he may have died here in 1406. The property was bought by Sir William Cochrane in 1636, and he used materials from the old castle to build the mansion of Auchans – itself now a ruin. Exhibition and visitor centre.

NOTE: [Tel: 01563 850201] Open daily April to September 10.00am-5.00pm. Managed by the Friends of Dundonald Castle.

P S R WC £

62 Dunfermline Palace and Abbey

Off A994, Dunfermline, Fife.

HS NT 089872 65 (Ref: H5)

Dunfermline Abbey was founded about 1070 by Queen Margaret, wife of Malcolm Canmore. Margaret was made a saint, and she and Malcolm were buried here. Abbot George Durie, the last abbot, removed their remains to the continent, where the Jesuits of Douai in Spain acquired her Margaret's head. Robert the Bruce's body (apart from his heart, which is at Melrose) is buried here. The Abbey was sacked in 1560, and fell into disrepair, although part of the church continued to be used.

There appears to have been a Royal Palace here from the 14th century, when Edward I stayed here in 1303-4. David II was born at the palace in 1323, but it may have been burned by Richard II in 1385. It was restored, and James I was born here in 1394. James IV, James V, and Mary, Queen of Scots, all visited. The Palace was remodelled in 1587 by Queen Anne, wife of James VI, and Charles I was born at the Palace in 1600. Charles II used the palace in 1650, but it was abandoned soon afterwards, and unroofed by 1708. The church, domestic buildings of the abbey, and the remains of the Royal Palace are open to the public. Exhibition.

NOTE: [Tel: 01383 739026]   Open daily all year except closed Thursday PM and Fridays October to March; choir of abbey church closed winter.

P Nearby S £

63 Dunnottar Castle

Off A92, 2 miles S of Stonehaven, Kincardine & Deeside.
Pri/LA   NO 882839   45   (Ref: F6)
Built on a promontory on cliffs high above the sea, Dunnottar Castle is a spectacular ruined courtyard castle, parts of which date from the 12th century. The castle consists of a 15th-

century L-plan keep, 16th- and 17th-century ranges around a large courtyard, as well as a chapel, stable block, forge, barracks, and priest's house.

Dunnottar was captured by William Wallace from the English in 1296, one story telling that he burnt 4000 Englishmen here. Edward III of England took the castle in the 1330s and strengthened it, but it was quickly recaptured by the Scots.

The Keith Earls Marischal acquired the property in 1382, and by the beginning of the 16th century Dunnottar was one of the strongest fortresses in Scotland. Mary, Queen of Scots, stayed here in 1562. The Marquis of Montrose unsuccessfully besieged it in 1645. In 1651 the Scottish crown jewels were brought here for safety, and Cromwell had the castle besieged in 1652. Before the garrison surrendered, after an eight month siege, the regalia and state papers were smuggled out to be hidden in nearby Kinneff Church until recovered at the Restoration.

In 1685 Covenanters, numbering some 167 women and men, were packed into one of the cellars during a hot summer and nine died while 25 escaped. The others, when freed, were found to have been tortured. The Earl Marischal supported the Jacobites in the Rising of 1715, and was forfeited. The castle was partly dismantled in 1716, and again in 1718, and became ruinous.

External shots of the castle were used in the film *Hamlet* with Mel Gibson. Getting to the castle involves a walk, steep climb, and a steeper one back.

NOTE: [Tel: 01569 762173]   Open Easter weekend to October Monday to Saturday 9.00am-6.00pm; Sunday 2.00-5.00pm; winter open Monday to Friday 9.00am to sunset, closed at weekends.

64 Dunrobin Castle

Off A9, 1.5 miles NE of Golspie, Sutherland.
Pri/LA   NC 852008   17   (Ref: C5)

Dunrobin, an elegant mansion designed like a fairytale castle, consists of an altered keep, which may date from the 1300s, and 17th-century courtyard mansion. The castle was remodelled and extended around 1780, between 1845 and 1851 by Sir Charles Barry, and again in 1915-21 by Sir Robert Lorimer.

The Sutherland family were created Earls of Sutherland in 1235, and had a castle here in the 13th century, and Dunrobin may be called after Robert or Robin, the 6th Earl. The property passed by marriage to the Gordons. Collections of furniture, paintings and memorabilia. Formal gardens. Museum.

The upper floors of the castle are reputedly haunted by the spectre of a daughter of the 14th Earl. She decided to elope with her lover but her father, who considered the man unsuitable for his daughter, found out, and had her imprisoned in one of the attic rooms. She tried to escape by climbing down a rope, from one of the upstairs windows, but her father surprised her, and she fell to her death. It is said that the one of the rooms she haunts has since been disused.

NOTE: [Tel: 01408 633268]   Open daily 1 April to 15 October.

65 Dunstaffnage Castle

Off A85, 3.5 miles NE of Oban, Argyll.
HS   NM 882344   49   (Ref: G3)

On a promontory in the Firth of Lorn, Dunstaffnage Castle consists of a massive and tall 13th-century curtain wall, with round towers, and a 16th-century gatehouse, which was later much altered and is still roofed. Ruinous ranges of buildings contained a hall and kitchen.

A stronghold here was held by the kings of Dalriada in the 7th century, and was one of the places that the Stone of Destiny was kept. The present castle was built by the MacDougalls. The castle was besieged and captured by Robert the Bruce in 1309, and Bruce made the castle a royal property, with the Campbells as keepers. James IV visited twice. In 1715 and 1746 government troops occupied the castle during the Jacobite Risings, and Flora MacDonald was briefly imprisoned here after helping Bonnie Prince Charlie. The castle was put into the care

of the State in 1958, and there is a fine ruined chapel nearby.

The castle is said to be haunted by a ghost in a green dress, the 'Ell-maid of Dunstaffnage' and her appearance heralds events, both bad and good, in the lives of the Campbells. She is said to be a *Glaistig*, a fairy woman.

NOTE: [Tel: 01631 562465]   Open daily all year except closed Thursday PM and Friday October to March.

P S WC £

66 Dunvegan Castle

Off A850, 1 mile N of the village of Dunvegan, Skye.
Pri/LA NG 247491 23 (Ref: D2)

Dunvegan Castle consists of a massive 14th-century keep, a 15th-century tower – the Fairy Tower – and a joining hall block from the 17th century. The castle was completely remodelled, with ornamental turrets and modern battlements, in the 19th century.

It was a property of the MacLeods from the 13th century. The castle is the home of the 'Fairy

Flag', reputedly given to one of the chiefs by his fairy wife. The flag reportedly gives victory to Clan MacLeod whenever unfurled, and is said to have done so both at the battles of Glendale in 1490 and Trumpan, after the MacDonalds had slaughtered many of the MacLeods at the church there, in 1580. It was also said to make the marriage of the MacLeods fruitful, when draped on the nuptial bed, and to charm the herrings in the loch.

Another interesting item is a drinking horn, Rory Mor's Horn, holding several pints, which the heir of the MacLeods had to empty in one go. There are mementoes of Bonnie Prince Charlie and Flora MacDonald. Exhibition. Garden. Boat trips. Disabled WC.

NOTE: [Tel: 01470 521206]   Open daily 23 March to 31 October 10.00-5.30pm; November to March 11.00-4.00pm.

P S R WC £

67 Earl's Palace, Birsay

Off A966, 12 miles N of Stromness, Orkney.

HS HY 248279 6 (Ref: A5)

Once a fine and stately building, the Earl's Palace at Birsay is a ruined 16th-century courtyard castle, started by Robert Stewart, Earl of Orkney about 1574 and completed by his son, Patrick Stewart, before 1614. Father and son oppressed the islanders, and taxed them to pay for the palace at Birsay and at Kirkwall. Earl Patrick was charged with treason and executed in 1615 after his son, Robert, had led a rising. Robert shared the fate of his father.

Nearby [HY 239285] on an island is the Brough of Birsay, an early Christian settlement, which was later used by Norsemen, and became an important centre. Earl Thorfinn of Orkney had a house here, and there was a substantial 12th-century church. The island is reached by a causeway, which floods at high tide.

NOTE: Open all year.

68 Earl's Palace, Kirkwall

On A960, in Kirkwall , Orkney.

HS HY 449107 6 (Ref: A6)

The Earl's Palace is a ruinous 17th-century U-plan palace, consisting of a main block, one long projecting wing, and another small offset square wing. The building is dominated by large oriel windows.

The palace was built by Patrick Stewart, Earl of Orkney, the illegitimate half-brother of Mary, Queen of Scots. He oppressed the Orcadians, and was imprisoned in 1609. His son led a rebellion in the islands in 1614, capturing the Palace and Kirkwall Castle, as well as Earl's Palace at Birsay. The rising was put down, and Patrick and Robert Stewart were both executed in Edinburgh in 1615. The Bishops of Orkney occupied the palace until 1688. (Also see Bishop's Palace). The fine medieval cathedral stands nearby.

NOTE: [Tel: 01856 875461]   Open April to September.

P Nearby S £

69 Edinburgh Castle

Off A1, in the centre of Edinburgh.

HS NT 252735 66 (Ref: H5)

Standing on a high rock, Edinburgh Castle was one of the strongest and most important fortresses in Scotland. The oldest building is a small Norman chapel of the early 12th century, dedicated to St Margaret, wife of Malcolm Canmore.

The castle had an English garrison from 1296 until 1313 during the Wars of Independence, when the Scots, led by Thomas Randolph, climbed the rock, surprised the garrison, and retook it. The castle was slighted, but there was an English garrison here again until 1341, when it was retaken by a Scot's force disguised as merchants. In 1367-71 David II rebuilt the castle with strong curtain walls and towers, and a large L-plan keep, David's Tower, which was named after him.

After the murder of the young Earl of Douglas and his brother at the 'Black Dinner' at the castle in 1440, it was attacked and captured by the Douglases after a nine month siege, and required substantial repairs. In 1566 Mary, Queen of Scots, gave birth to the future James VI in the castle. After her abdication, it was held on her behalf, until English help forced it to surrender in 1573.

The castle was captured in 1640 after a three-month siege by the Covenanters, and Cromwell besieged it throughout the autumn of 1650. The Jacobites failed to take it in both the 1715 and 1745 Risings.

The castle is the home of the Scottish Crown Jewels, and the Stone of Destiny – on which the Kings of Scots were inaugurated – and is an interesting complex of buildings with spectacular views over the capital. Visitors with a disability can be taken to the top of the castle by a courtesy vehicle; ramps and lift access to Crown Jewels and Stone of Destiny. Disabled facilities and WC.

NOTE: [Tel: 0131 225 9846] Open daily all year.

P Nearby S R WC £

70 Edzell Castle

Off B966, 6 miles N of Brechin, Angus.

HS NO 585693 44 (Ref: F6)

Edzell Castle consists of an early 16th-century tower house, later enlarged and extended with ranges of buildings around a courtyard, all now ruinous. A large pleasance, or garden, was created in 1604, and was surrounded by an ornamental wall, to which a summerhouse and a

bathhouse were added. The fine carved decoration of the garden walls was unique.

The castle was built by the Lindsay Earls of Crawford. Mary, Queen of Scots, stayed here in 1562, and Cromwell garrisoned it in 1651. The Lindsays had to sell the property in 1715, because of huge debts, and it was bought by the Maule Earl of Panmure. The Maules were forfeited for their part in the 1745 Jacobite Rising, and the castle was garrisoned by Hanoverian troops, who did much damage. The Maules recovered Edzell in 1764, but the castle was abandoned soon afterwards. It later passed to the Earl of Dalhousie, and was put into the care of the State in the 1930s.

One story associated with the castle is that the one of the Lindsay lairds was cursed by a gypsy woman, after he had hanged her sons for poaching. The tales goes that his pregnant wife died that day, while he himself was devoured by wolves – as foretold.

Exhibition. Garden. Reasonable disabled access and WC.

NOTE: [Tel: 01356 648631]   Open daily all year except closed Thursday PM and Fridays October to March.

P S WC £

71 Eilean Donan Castle

On A87, 8 miles E of Kyle of Lochalsh, Highland.
Pri/LA NG 881259 33 (E3)

One of the most beautifully situated of all Scottish castles, Eilean Donan Castle consists of a 13th-century wall, surrounding a courtyard, with a strong 14th-century keep. Adjoining ranges of outbuildings and fortifications were added in later centuries. Although very ruinous, it was completely rebuilt in the 20th century.

Alexander III gave the lands to Colin Fitzgerald, son of the Irish Earl of Desmond and Kildare, for his help in defeating King Haakon and his Norsemen at the Battle of Largs in 1263. The family changed their name to Mackenzie, and Eilean Donan became their main stronghold. Robert the Bruce sheltered here in 1306.

In 1331 Randolph, Earl of Moray, executed 50 men at Eilean Donan and 'decorated' the castle walls with their heads; and in 1509 the MacRaes became constables of the castle. In 1539 it was besieged by Donald Gorm MacDonald, a claimant to the Lordship of the Isles, but he was killed by an arrow shot from the castle.

William Mackenzie, 5th Earl of Seaforth, had it garrisoned with Spanish troops during the Jacobite rising of 1719, but three Hanoverian frigates battered it into submission with cannon, and it was blown up from within. The ghost of one of the Spanish troops, killed either at the castle or the nearby battle of Glenshiel, is said to haunt the castle. Visitor centre to open in summer. Mementoes of Bonnie Prince Charlie and James III. New exhibitions. Disabled WC.

NOTE: [Tel: 01599 555202]   Open 1 April or Easter to end October.

P S R WC £

72 Elcho Castle

Off A912, 3 miles SE of Perth.

HS NO 165211 58 (Ref: G5)

Both stronghold and comfortable residence, Elcho Castle is a 16th-century Z-plan tower house, with a long rectangular main block and several towers.

William Wallace is supposed to have sheltered here, but nothing of this early castle remains. The Wemyss family held the property from 1468, and were made Lords Elcho in 1633. David, Lord Elcho, fought and survived the Battle of Culloden on the Jacobite side in 1746, but had to flee to France. By the 1780s, Elcho Castle was abandoned and fell into decay, but it was reroofed in 1830. It has been in the care of the State since 1929.

NOTE: [Tel: 01738 639998]   Open April to September.

P Nearby S WC £

73 Falkland Palace

Off A912, 4 miles N of Glenrothes, Fife.

NTS NO 254075 59 (Ref: G5)

A fortified but comfortable residence remodelled in Renaissance style, Falkland Palace consists of ranges of buildings around an open courtyard. The late 15th-century gatehouse range survives complete, while an adjoining range is ruined, and only traces remain of a range opposite the gatehouse.

The Chapel Royal, with fine mullioned windows, has a 16th-century oak screen at one end, and the painted ceiling dates from 1633. There is also a fine tapestry gallery, and access to the keeper's apartments. The restored cross house contains a refurbished room, reputedly the King's Room, where James V died in 1542.

Falkland was used as a hunting seat by the kings of Scots from the 12th century. The property was owned by the MacDuff Earls of Fife in the 14th century, and the castle was destroyed by the English in 1337. It was rebuilt, and in 1371 passed to Robert Stewart, Duke of Albany. He had David, Duke of Rothesay, his nephew and the heir of Robert III, imprisoned here and starved to death in 1402.

After 1425 Falkland was acquired by the Crown, and was used by Mary, wife of James II, and it became a favourite residence of the Stewart kings. It was used and remodelled by James III, James IV, and James V. Mary, Queen of Scots, visited the palace in 1563, James VI stayed at Falkland, as did Charles I in 1633, and Charles II in the 1650s. Despite a visit by George IV in 1822, the palace deteriorated until 1887 when it was restored by the 3rd Marquis of Bute. In

1952 The National Trust for Scotland assumed responsibility for the building.

There are extensive gardens and a Royal tennis court, dating from 1539. Visitor centre.

NOTE: [Tel: 01337 857397] Open daily April to October.

`P Nearby S WC £`

Falkland Palace

74 Fasque House

Off B974, 5 miles NW of Laurencekirk,
Kincardine & Deeside.
Pri/LA NO 648755 45 (Ref: F6)

The present castellated mansion was built in 1809, and passed to the Gladstones in 1829, one of whom, William Ewart Gladstone, became Prime Minister. William Gladstone library, kitchen, and family church. Deer park and walks. Disabled access to ground floor.

NOTE: [Tel: 01561 340202/215] Open May to September 11.00-5.30pm.

`P S R WC £`

75 Ferniehirst Castle

Off A68, 1.5 miles S of Jedburgh, Borders.
Pri/LA NT 653179 80 (Ref:I6)

Ferniehirst Castle consists of an extended and altered tower house, which incorporates the cellars from the 16th-century castle, with later wings and extensions. The original entrance leads to a stair known as the 'Left-Handed Staircase', the story being that when Sir Andrew Kerr, who was himself left-handed, returned from Flodden in 1513 he had his followers trained to use their weapons with their left hands. This is said to be the origin of 'Corrie-fisted' or 'Kerr-handed'. The castle was taken and sacked by the English in 1523, but was recaptured with French help in 1549, and the leader of the English garrison beheaded. Sir Thomas Kerr, protector of Mary, Queen of Scots, invaded England in 1570, hoping to have her released, but all that resulted was an raid on Scotland, during which Ferniehirst was damaged. James VI attacked the castle in 1593, because of help given by the family to the Earl of Bothwell, and the castle was rebuilt about 1598. Collection of portraits. Turret library.

NOTE: [Tel: 01835 862201] Open daily July 11.00am-4.00pm, except Mondays.

`P S WC £`

76 Finlaggan
Off A846, 3 miles W of Port Askaig, Islay.
Ruin NR 388681 60 (Ref: H2)
Little remains of Finlaggan, except foundations on two islands. Remains have recently been found of a 15th-century keep on the smaller or council island. The ruins of a chapel and many other buildings stand on the larger island, Eilean Mor.

There was a kingdom of the Isles, subject to Norway, from about 900. In the 12th century, Somerled, of mixed Norse and Celtic blood, pushed the Norsemen out of much of Scotland and took control of their territories. He was assassinated at Renfrew in 1164 when at war Malcolm IV. He was succeeded by his sons Reginald in Kintyre and Islay; Dugald in Lorn, Mull and Jura; and Angus in Bute, Arran and North Argyll.

The whole area became part of the kingdom of Scots in 1266 after the Battle of Largs in 1263. Angus Og MacDonald – grandson of Donald, a son of Reginald: hence MacDonald – a friend and supporter of Robert the Bruce, died at Finlaggan in 1328, and his son, John of Islay, was the first to use the title 'Lord of the Isles'. The independence of the Lords, however, and their power and influence, caused constant trouble for the kings of Scots. A campaign by the 2nd Lord led to the bloody Battle of Harlaw in 1411, and the 3rd Lord was twice imprisoned by James I. James IV eventually destroyed the power of the Lords in a campaign in 1493, and had the John, the then Lord of the Isles, imprisoned until his death in 1503. Attempts were made to restore the Lordship, but these were ultimately unsuccessful. Visitor centre near the island.
NOTE: Closed in winter – boat out to island.

P Nearby S

77 Finlaystone House
On A8, 3 miles E of Port Glasgow, Renfrewshire.
Pri/LA NS 367738 63 (Ref: H4)
Finlaystone House, a grand symmetrical mansion mostly dating from 1760 and later, was remodelled between 1898 and 1903. The building incorporates a 15th-century castle of the Cunningham Earls of Glencairn. The 5th Earl had John Knox preach here in 1556, and fought against Mary, Queen of Scots, at the Battle of Carberry Hill in 1567. The 9th Earl led a rising for Charles II against Cromwell in 1654; and, although the rebellion was a failure, after the Restoration he was made Chancellor of Scotland. Robert Burns – who was friends with the then Earl – also visited the house. Finlaystone later passed to the MacMillans. Visitor centre with Clan MacMillan exhibits, doll museum, and Celtic art display. Gardens. Disabled access to ground floor and grounds. WC.
NOTE: [Tel: 01475 540285] House open Sundays PM April to August; gardens and grounds open all year.

P S R WC £

78 Floors Castle
Off A6089, 1 mile NW of Kelso, Borders.
Pri/LA NT 711346 74 (Ref: H6)
The largest inhabited mansion in Scotland, the present house consists of a large towered and turreted central block with other wings and ranges. The building dates from 1721, and was designed by William Adam for the 1st Duke of Roxburghe. The house was remodelled in the 19th century with a profusion of spires and domes, corbelling and battlements, to the designs of William Playfair.

Floors is still the home of the Duke and Duchess of Roxburghe, and was used in the film

Greystoke. Collections of furniture, tapestries, works of art and porcelain. Walled garden and park. Disabled access to house; lift for wheelchairs; WC.

NOTE: [Tel: 01573 223333]   Open Easter to end October 10.00am-4.30pm

P S R WC £

79 Fort George

Off B9006, 10 miles NE of Inverness, Highland.
HS NH 763566 27 (Ref: D5)
Fort George is an magnificent massive Georgian artillery fort. It was built after the Jacobite rising of 1745-6 to designs of William Skinner, but was not completed until 1769, by which time it was not needed. Many of the buildings were designed by William and John Adam. It

extends over 16 acres and could accommodate nearly 2000 men; and is still used as a barracks. Reconstruction of barrack rooms in different periods, and a display of muskets and pikes. Reasonable disabled access and WC.

NOTE: [Tel: 01667 462777]   Open all year.

P S R WC £

80 Fyvie Castle

Off A947 1 mile N of Fyvie village, Banff & Buchan.
NTS NJ 764393 29 (Ref: D6)
One of the most splendid castles in Scotland, Fyvie Castle consists of a large L-plan tower house with very long wings. The main block is known as the Seton Tower, and three large towers, the Preston, Meldrum and Gordon towers, each refer to the family which built it. The building is adorned with fine corbelling, turrets, steep corbiestepped roofs and dormer windows. There are also many original interiors.

Fyvie was originally a property of the Lindsays. William the Lyon held court here in 1214, as did Alexander II in 1222. Edward I of England stayed in 1296, during the Wars of Independence, then Robert the Bruce in 1308.

The property passed to the Prestons, then to the Meldrums between 1440 and 1596, then the Seton Earls of Dunfermline. The Marquis of Montrose occupied the castle in 1644, and in the 1650s it was held by a Cromwellian force. It passed to the Gordons in the 18th century, and later to the Leith family, who extended the castle further in 1890. It is now owned by The National Trust for Scotland. Collections of portraits, arms and armour and tapestries. Grounds. Disabled WC.

The castle is said to be haunted by a 'Green Lady', the spectre of Lilias Drummond, wife of Alexander Seton, who died in 1601. Her appearance bodes ill for the family. She may have been starved to death by her husband, who remarried quickly after her death. The ghost is said to have scratched her name on the window sill of the newlyweds' bedroom soon after they were married – and the writing can still be seen.

NOTE: [Tel: 01651 891266]   Open April to September and weekends only in October. Grounds open all year.

P   S   R   WC   £

81 Glamis Castle

Off A928, 5.5 miles SW of Forfar, Angus.
Pri/LA NO 387481 54 (Ref: G6)

One of the most famous and reputedly haunted, castles in Scotland, Glamis Castle consists of a greatly extended 14th-century keep. It was altered to an L-plan in the 16th century, and the battlements were replaced with turrets and dormers. It was extended again, with lower wings and round towers, in the 17th, 18th and 19th centuries.

In the 15th century the lands were held by Sir John Lyon, Chancellor of Scotland, who married a daughter of Robert II. The family were made Lords Glamis in 1445. In 1540 the young and beautiful wife of the 6th Lord, Janet Douglas, was burned to death for witchcraft by James V, who hated the Douglases. Mary, Queen of Scots, stayed here in 1562.

The castle is still held by the Lyons, now Earls of Strathmore and Kinghorne, and the present Queen Mother comes from this family. Collections of historic pictures, porcelain and furniture. Extensive park, nature trail and garden. Two additional exhibition rooms. Four shops and restaurant. Disabled access to gardens and ground floor; WC.

The castle is reputedly one the most haunted in Britain. The ghost of Alexander Lindsay, 4th Earl of Crawford, 'Earl Beardie', is said to haunt a walled-up room where he played cards with the devil. Another ghost is the 'Grey Lady of Glamis', the ghost of Janet Douglas, who was burnt by James V. The apparition of a little African boy is said to sit on a stone seat in the hall.

NOTE: [Tel: 01307 840393]   Open 29 March to 25 October 10.30am-5.30pm (from 10.00am July and August); last tour 4.45pm.

P   S   R   WC   £

82 Glenbuchat Castle

Off A97, 13 miles W of Alford, Aberdeenshire.
HS NJ 397149 37 (Ref: E6)

Glenbuchat Castle is a roofless, but otherwise complete, late 16th-century Z-plan tower house. Round and square turrets crown the corners of the tower. The castle was built by the Gordons. It was occupied by James VI's forces in 1592 during the Catholic rebellion of the Gordon Earl of Huntly. Brigadier-General John Gordon of Glenbuchat fought for the Jacobites in both the 1715 and 1745 Risings, and led the Gordons and Farquharsons at the Battle of Culloden in 1746 – when already 70. He managed to escape to Norway, disguised as a beggar, and died in France. The castle was a ruin by 1738, and later sold to the Duff Earl of Fife.

NOTE: Open all year.

P

83 Greenknowe Tower

On A6105, 0.5 miles W of Gordon, Borders.

HS NT 639428 74 (Ref: H6)

Built for comfort as well as defence, Greenknowe Tower is a 16th-century L-plan tower house, with turrets crowning the corners of the building. The entrance, in the re-entrant angle, still has an iron yett.

Greenknowe passed by marriage from the Gordons to the Setons of Touch, who built the tower. In the 17th century it was acquired by the Pringles of Stichel, and was occupied until the middle of the 19th century. It was put into the care of the State in 1937.

NOTE: Open all year.

P Nearby

84 Haddo House

Off B9005, 10 miles NW of Ellon, Aberdeenshire.

NTS NJ 868347 30 (Ref: D6)

Haddo House, a fine classical mansion with two sweeping wings, was built in 1731-6 by the architect William Adam for William Gordon, 2nd Earl of Aberdeen. Exhibition of paintings. Disabled access to house and grounds.

Nothing survives of an old castle of the Gordons, who had held the lands from 1429. In 1644 Sir John Gordon of Haddo, who had fought in the army of the Marquis of Montrose, was captured after being besieged in the old castle for three days. He was imprisoned in 'Haddo's Hole' in St Giles Cathedral before being executed by beheading. The castle was then destroyed.

NOTE: [Tel: 01651 851440]   Open Easter weekend, then daily May to September, weekends only in October. Garden and country park open all year.

P S R WC £

Hailes Castle – see next page

85 Hailes Castle

Off A1, 1.5 miles W of East Linton, East Lothian.
HS   NT 575758   67   (Ref: H6)
In a lovely location above a river, Hailes Castle consists of a 14th-century keep, extended by
ranges and towers in the 15th and 16th centuries, within a thick 13th-century curtain wall. The
castle had a large courtyard, fragments of which remain.

Hailes was a Hepburn property, having passed from the Cospatrick Earl of Dunbar and March,
and the de Gourlay family. Archibald Dunbar captured the castle in 1443, and slew all he
found within in the walls. Patrick Hepburn became Earl of Bothwell, but was killed at the
Battle of Flodden in 1513. The castle was burnt in 1532, and in 1547 was occupied by Lord
Gray of Wilton for the English. James Hepburn, 4th Earl of Bothwell, brought Mary, Queen of
Scots, here after abducting her in 1567, and they married soon afterwards. In 1650 the castle
was partly dismantled by Cromwell. It passed to the Stewarts, then the Setons, who in 1700
sold the castle to the Dalrymples of Hailes, but was then abandoned for the mansion of New
Hailes, near Musselburgh. In 1835 Hailes was being used as a granary, but in 1926 was transferred
into State care.
NOTE: Open all year.

P Nearby

86 Hermitage Castle

Off B6357, 5 miles N of Newcastleton, Borders.
HS   NY 497960   79   (Ref: I6)
One of the most impressive and oppressive of Scottish fortresses, Hermitage Castle consists
of a 13th-century courtyard and large 14th-century keep of four storeys, around which has
been constructed a massive castle. In the 15th century a new rectangular wing was extended
from the main keep.

The property belonged to the Dacres, but passed to the De Soulis family. One of the family
was a man of ill repute and said to dabble in witchcraft. Many local children were apparently
seized by Soulis and never seen again. The local people, according to one story, eventually
rebelled and Soulis was wrapped in lead and boiled in a cauldron, although he may actually
have been imprisoned in Dumbarton Castle for supporting the English. The family were
forfeited in 1320.

The castle passed to the Grahams, then by marriage to the Douglas family. William Douglas,
'The Knight of Liddlesdale', was prominent in resisting Edward Balliol in 1330s. He seized Sir
Alexander Ramsay of Dalhousie, however, while at his devotions, imprisoned him in a dungeon
at the castle, and starved him to death. In 1353 Douglas was murdered by his godson, another
William Douglas, after he had tried to block his claim to the lordship of Douglas.

In 1492 Archibald, 5th Earl of Angus, was forced to exchange Hermitage for Bothwell with
Patrick Hepburn, Earl of Bothwell. In 1566 James Hepburn, 4th Earl of Bothwell, was badly
wounded in a skirmish with the Border reiver 'Little Jock' Elliot of Park, and was paid a visit on
his sick bed by Mary, Queen of Scots, who had ridden all the way from Jedburgh. The castle
and title passed from the Hepburns to Francis Stewart, Earl of Bothwell, then to the Scotts of
Buccleuch about 1600. The castle was partly restored in the 19th century.
NOTE: [Tel: 01387 376222]   Open daily April to September.

P   S

87 Hill of Tarvit Mansion House

Off A916, 2 miles S of Cupar, Fife.

NTS NO 380119 59 (Ref: G6)

The original house, dating from 1696 with 19th-century wings, was virtually rebuilt in 1906. It was remodelled by the architect Sir Robert Lorimer for Mr F. B. Sharp to house fine collections of paintings and pictures, furniture, Flemish tapestries and Chinese porcelain and bronzes. Formal gardens. Restored Edwardian laundry. Woodland walk. Scotstarvit Tower is nearby. Limited disabled access to house; WC.

NOTE: [Tel: 01334 653127] Open Easter weekend; open May to September; open weekends only in October; grounds open all year.

P S R WC £

88 Hollows Tower

Off A7, 2 miles N of Canonbie, Dumfries & Galloway.

Pri/LA NY 383787 85 (Ref: I6)

Situated on a strong site, Hollows Tower is a rectangular 16th-century tower house. It was a stronghold of the unruly Armstrongs after nearby Gilnockie Castle had been destroyed in 1523 by the English. Johnnie Armstrong of Gilnockie was hanged without trial by James V in 1530, with 50 of his family. The tower has been reroofed and restored, and is now occupied by the Clan Armstrong Centre.

NOTE: [Tel: 01387 371876] Guided tours – check opening.

P S WC £

89 Holyroodhouse

Off A1, in Edinburgh.

Pri/LA NT 269739 66 (Ref: H5)

Holyroodhouse consists of ranges of buildings surrounding a rectangular courtyard, one of which dates from the 16th century, and was built out of the guest house of the Abbey. The palace was rebuilt in the late 17th century, a new block being built to balance the original range. The building was remodelled and extended by Sir William Bruce for Charles II in 1671-8. Original 16th-century interiors survive in the old block, and the ruins of the abbey church adjoin.

Holyrood Abbey was

founded by David I around 1128 although it was sacked in 1322 and 1385 by the English. James III found the guest range of the abbey a comfortable alternative to Edinburgh castle, and James IV and James V extended the building. The English burnt the abbey in 1544 and 1547. David Rizzio, Mary, Queen of Scots's secretary was murdered here in her presence by men including her husband, Lord Darnley. Bonnie Prince Charlie stayed here in 1745. The palace is the official residence of the monarch in Scotland. Fine interiors. Collections of pictures and furniture.

NOTE: [Tel: 0131 556 1096]   Open all year except when monarch is in residence, Good Friday, and 25/26 December.

Nearby S £

90 Hopetoun House

Off A904, 2.5 miles W of Forth Road Bridge, West Lothian
Pri/LA NT 089790 65 (Ref: H5)

The large and stately palatial mansion, with a central block and flanking wings, dates from 1699, and was built by the architect William Bruce for the Hope family. Sir Charles Hope was made Earl of Hopetoun in 1703, and had the house remodelled by William Adam from 1721, the work being continued by John and Robert Adam. Fine interiors. Collections of furniture and pictures. Exhibitions. Park land.

NOTE: [Tel: 0131 331 2451]   Open daily 10 April to 27 September 10.00-5.30pm

P S R WC £

91 House of Dun

Off A935, 3 miles NW of Montrose, Angus.
NTS NO 670599 54 (Ref: F6)

The present House of Dun, a fine classical mansion, was built in 1730 by the architect William Adam for David Erskine Lord Dun. The Erskine family held the lands from 1375, and had a castle here. One of the family was John Erskine, a scholar and reformer in the time of Mary, Queen of Scots. Fine plasterwork and a collection of portraits, furniture and porcelain. Walled garden and handloom weaving workshop. Disabled access and WC.

NOTE: [Tel: 01674 810264]   Open Easter weekend, then daily May to September; open weekends in October. Garden and grounds open all year. Coaches by appointment only.

R WC £

92 Huntingtower Castle

Off A85, 3 miles NW of Perth.
HS NO 083252 58 (Ref: G5)

A well-preserved and interesting castle, Huntingtower consists of a 15th-century keep, a nearby but not touching 16th-century L-plan tower house, and a later small connecting range. Some rooms have fine painted ceilings, wall paintings, and there are decorative beams in the hall.

The property was held by the Ruthvens from the 12th century, and was originally called Ruthven Castle. Mary, Queen of Scots, visited the castle in 1565. In 1582 the 4th Lord Ruthven, who had been made Earl of Gowrie in 1581, kidnapped the young James VI – in the 'Raid of Ruthven'. James was held at Huntingtower for a year until he escaped during a hunting trip. The Earl was beheaded in 1585.

The Ruthvens were forfeited for treason in 1600 after the 'Gowrie Conspiracy' – a plot to murder James VI – their name proscribed, and the castle renamed Huntingtower.

Huntingtower passed to the Murray Dukes of Atholl. The Jacobite general Lord George Murray was born here; but by the 19th-century Huntingtower was used to house labourers. It was put into the care of the State in 1912.

The space between the battlements of the two towers is known as 'The Maiden's Leap'. A daughter of the 1st Earl of Gowrie is said to have jumped from one tower to the other. While visiting her lover in his chamber, and about to be discovered by her mother, she leapt to the other tower and returned to her own bed before her mother caught her. She eloped with her lover the following night.

The castle and grounds are said to be haunted by a 'Green Lady'.

NOTE: [Tel: 01738 627231]   Open daily all year except closed Thursday PM and Fridays October to March.

P S £

93 Huntly Castle

Off A920, N of Huntly, Aberdeenshire.

HS NJ 532407 29 (Ref: D6)

A fine building with a long and violent history, Huntly Castle consists of a strong 15th-century keep, rectangular in plan, with an adjoining large courtyard which had ranges of buildings on two sides, all now ruinous.

An older castle here, called Strathbogie, was built by the MacDuff Earls of Fife on a nearby motte, and passed to the Gordons early in the 14th century. Robert the Bruce stayed here before defeating the Comyn Earl of Buchan in 1307. This old castle was burned down in 1452, and a new castle was built close by. In 1506 the name was changed from Strathbogie to Huntly after the family were made Earls.

The 4th Earl of Huntly was defeated – and then died, reportedly from apoplexy – by the forces of Mary, Queen of Scots, at the Battle of Corrichie in 1562, and his son was executed. The castle was slighted and plundered at this time.

The castle was restored, but in 1594 was attacked by James VI and damaged again after another rebellion by the then Earl. It was restored once again in 1602. The 2nd Marquis of Huntly was

hanged for his support of Charles I, and in 1640 the castle was occupied by a Covenanters. In 1644 it was taken by forces of the Marquis of Montrose, but was captured by General David Leslie in 1647 after starving out and slaughtering the garrison. It was held by Hanoverian soldiers, during the Jacobite rising of 1745-6, but by then had been abandoned as a residence and. It was then used as a quarry and dump until cleared in 1923. Exhibition.

NOTE: [Tel: 01466 793191]   Open daily all year except closed Thursday PM and Fridays October to March.

P S WC £

94 Inveraray Castle

Off A83, N of Inveraray, Argyll
Pri/LA NN 096093 56 (Ref: G4)

Inveraray Castle, a large classical mansion with corner towers and turrets, was begun in 1744. It was remodelled by William and John Adam; then again in 1877 after a fire. The castle, which is the seat of the Dukes of Argyll, houses many interesting rooms, with collections of tapestries and paintings, and superb displays of weapons. Other items of interest include Rob Roy MacGregor's sporran and dirk handle. Clan Room features information of special interest to members of Clan Campbell.

Nearby, but now demolished, was the 15th-century castle of the Campbells. James V visited in 1533, as did Mary, Queen of Scots, in 1562. This castle was burnt in 1644 by the Marquis of Montrose, and was demolished as part of the 3rd Duke of Argyll's rebuilding of the present castle and town of Inveraray.

NOTE: [Tel: 01499 302203]   Open 1st Saturday April to 2nd Sunday October Saturday-Thursday; July and August daily.

P S R WC £

95 Inverlochy Castle

Off A82, 1.5 miles NE of Fort William, Highland.
HS NN 120754 41 (Ref: F4)
Inverlochy Castle is a ruined 13th-century castle of enclosure, with a round tower at each corner, of the Comyns of Badenoch. There were two entrances, opposite each other, with portcullises.

The Comyns were destroyed by Robert the Bruce around 1308, and the castle was later held by the Gordons of Huntly. Major consolidation work is underway.

Fort William is named after the nearby ruinous fort, which was built by General Monck for Cromwell during the 1650s, then reconstructed and renamed in 1690, during the reign of William of Orange. It was bombarded in the spring of 1746 by Jacobites, but could not be taken. It was garrisoned until 1866, after which most of it was demolished.

NOTE: Inverlochy Castle open all year – view from exterior for present.

P

96 Kelburn Castle

Off A78, 2 miles S of Largs, Ayrshire.
Pri/LA NS 217567 63 (Ref: H4)
Kelburn Castle is a tall 16th-century tower house, although part may date from the 13th century, to which has been added a large symmetrical mansion. The castle was extended in 1700, and again in 1879.

The Boyles held the lands of Kelburn from the 13th century, and John Boyle of Kelburn, a supporter of James III, was killed at the Battle of Sauchieburn in 1488. The Boyles were made Earls of Glasgow and Viscounts Kelburn in 1703, for helping persuade reluctant Jacobites to sign to Act of Union. They still occupy the castle, making Kelburn one of the oldest houses continuously occupied by the same family. The grounds are open to the public as a Country Centre. Walled gardens.

NOTE: [Tel: 01475 586685]
Open daily July and August – tours; grounds open all year.

P S R WC £

97 Kellie Castle

Off B9171, 4 miles N of Elie, Fife.
NTS NO 520052 59 (Ref: G6)
One of the finest castles in Scotland, Kellie Castle is a tall 16th-century E-plan tower house, consisting of a three-storey main block and three large square towers which form the E. The Vine Room, on one of the upper floors, has a ceiling painted by De Witt, and there are fine plaster

Kellie Castle

ceilings elsewhere. There is a magnificent walled garden.

An earlier castle here belonged to the Siwards, but the present castle was built by the Oliphants, who held the lands from 1360 until 1613, when the 5th Lord Oliphant had to sell the property. It was bought by Sir Thomas Erskine of Gogar, who was made Earl of Kellie in 1619, a favourite of James VI.

Kellie was abandoned in 1829, but in 1878 James Lorimer leased Kellie as an almost roofless ruin and proceeded to restore it. Robert Lorimer, his son, spent most of his childhood at Kellie, and was a famous architect. In 1970 Kellie passed into the care of The National Trust for Scotland. Limited disabled access to house.

NOTE: [Tel: 01333 720271] Open Easter weekend; May to September; open weekends in October. Grounds open all year.

P S R WC £

98 Kiessimul Castle

Off A888 S of Castlebay, Barra.

Pri/LA NL 665979 31 (Ref: E1)

Kiessimul Castle consists of curtain wall shaped to fit the island on which it stands, enclosing a keep, hall and other ranges of buildings.

Although Clan MacNeil claim descent from Neil of the Nine Hostages, High King of Ireland at the end of the 4th century, the first to settle in Scotland seems to have been Hugh, King of Aileachh and Prince of Argyll. His son, 21st in descent, was called Neil of the Castle, and built a stronghold here in 1030, or so it is claimed. The castle was besieged several times during clan battles. The family was forced to sell Barra to the Gordons of Cluny in 1840, but the castle was bought back in 1937, and restored in the 1950s and 60s.

NOTE: [Tel: 01871 810449] Open April to October Monday, Wednesday & Saturday afternoons – wind and tide permitting. Open at other times by arrangement.

99 Kilchurn Castle

Off A85, 2 miles W of Dalmally, Argyll.

HS NN 133276 50 (Ref: G4)

A picturesque and much photographed ruin, Kilchurn Castle is a ruinous courtyard castle of the 15th century, consisting of a rectangular keep, which was extended with ranges of buildings in the 16th and 17th centuries.

The lands originally belonged to the MacGregors, but were acquired by the Campbells of Glenorchy, who built the castle. The castle was strengthened and improved by Black Duncan of the Seven Castles, Sir Duncan Campbell, at the end of the 16th century. The Campbells withstood a two-day siege in 1654 by General Middleton, before he retreated before Monck's Cromwellian forces. Kilchurn was inhabited by the Campbells until 1740, when they moved to Taymouth. The castle was garrisoned by Hanoverian troops in 1745, but was ruinous by 1770. The castle was put into the care of the state in 1953, and has been consolidated and repaired.

There are regular sailings from Loch Awe pier to Kilchurn by steamer – phone ferry company 01838 200400/200449.

NOTE: Open April to September.

P Nearby

100 Kildrummy Castle

Off A97, 10 miles W of Alford, Aberdeenshire.

HS   NJ 454164   37   (Ref: E6)

Although now ruinous, Kildrummy Castle, built in the 13th century, was one of the largest and most powerful early castles in Scotland. The high curtain walls enclosed a courtyard with six round towers at the corners and gate. One of these, the largest, called 'the Snow Tower', may have been the main keep.

The original castle was built by Gilbert de Moray in the 13th century. It was captured by Edward I of England in 1296, and then again in 1306 from a garrison led by Nigel Bruce, younger brother of Robert the Bruce, after the castle was set alight by a traitor. Nigel Bruce, and the rest of the garrison, were executed by hanging. The traitor was rewarded with much gold – poured molten down his throat.

The castle was restored before 1333, and besieged by the Earl of Atholl acting for the English in 1335. It was successfully defended by Bruce's sister, Christian. Her husband, Sir Andrew Moray, the Regent, relieved the castle and killed the Earl of Atholl. David II besieged it in 1363, and seized it from the Earl of Mar.

It was in royal hands from 1361-8, until Alexander Stewart, the Wolf of Badenoch, acquired it after he had forced Isabella Douglas, Countess of Mar, to marry him. It later passed to the Cochranes, then the Elphinstones from 1507-1626, until they were compelled to give it the Erskine Earls of Mar. It was also sacked in 1530 by the freebooter John Strachan of Lynturk; and was captured in 1654 by Cromwell's forces.

The castle was badly damaged in 1690, when it was burned by Jacobites, but was complete enough for 'Bobbing John' 6th Earl of Mar to use it as his base when he led the Jacobite Rising in 1715. After the collapse of the Jacobite cause, Kildrummy was deliberately dismantled, and then used as a quarry. It was put into the care of the State in 1951.

NOTE: [Tel: 01975 571331]   Open April to September.

P S WC £

101 Kilravock Castle

Off B9091, 6 miles SW of Nairn, Highland.

Pri/LA   NH 814493   27   (Ref: D5)

Pronounced 'Kilrock', Kilravock Castle is a plain massive 15th-century keep, to which has been added a tall 17th-century block, making the building L-plan, as well as other extensions.

The castle passed by marriage from the Bissets to the Roses of Kilravock in the 13th century, and they built the castle. Mary, Queen of Scots, visited the castle in 1562, and Hugh, the 16th laird, entertained Bonnie Prince Charlie here in 1746, then the Duke of Cumberland two days later. Robert Burns visited in 1787. The Rose family still occupy the castle.

NOTE: [Tel: 01667 493258]   Open Wednesday only April 27 to 3 October (1998); guided tours at 11.00 am, 2.00, 3.00 & 4.00pm.

P S R WC £

102 Kinnaird Head Castle

Off A92, N of Fraserburgh, Banff & Buchan.

HS   NJ 999677   30   (Ref: D7)

Kinnaird Head Castle consists of an altered massive 15th-century keep, rectangular in plan, the walls of which are harled and whitewashed. It was a property of the Frasers of Philorth. Sir Alexander Fraser built the harbour at Fraserburgh – the town was originally called Faithlie – came near to bankrupting himself, and had to sell much of his property in 1611. A lighthouse was built into the top of the castle in 1787, and the outbuildings were constructed around it in 1820 by Robert Stevenson, grandfather of Robert Louis Stevenson. The castle now forms part of a lighthouse museum. Disabled access to museum and toilet.

The Wine Tower, a lower tower, stands nearby. Sir Alexander Fraser is said to have had his daughter's lover, of whom he disapproved, chained in a sea cave below the building, where the poor man accidentally drowned. Fraser's daughter, Isobel, threw herself to her death on finding that her lover had been killed. An apparition is said to been seen by the Wine Tower whenever there is a storm.

NOTE: [Tel: 01346 511022]   Open daily all year as Lighthouse Museum – joint entry ticket.

P S R WC £

103 Lauriston Castle

Off B9085, 3 miles W of Edinburgh Castle.
Pri/LA NT 204762 66 (H5)

Lauriston Castle is a much-altered 16th-century tower house, to which was added a two-storey extension, designed by William Burn, in 1824-7. Two large pepperpot turrets crown one side.

The old castle was built by the Napiers of Merchiston, and one of the family, John Napier, was the inventor of logarithms. In 1656 the property was sold and it passed through many hands until coming to the Reids in 1902, the last owners, who gave it to the city of Edinburgh. The castle has a fine Edwardian-period interior, housing good collections of Italian furniture, Blue John, Grossley wool mosaics, Sheffield plate, mezzotint prints, Caucasian carpets, and items of decorative art.

NOTE: [Tel: 0131 336 2060]   Open April to October except Fridays; weekends only November to March; grounds open all year.

P WC £

104 Leith Hall

Off B9002, 3.5 miles NE of Rhynie, Aberdeenshire.

NTS   NJ 541298   37   (Ref: D6)

Leith Hall incorporates a 17th-century rectangular tower house, with turrets crowning the

corners. To this has been added 18th- and 19th-century blocks, to form four sides of a courtyard, with round towers. The walls are white-washed.

The Leith family held the property from 1650 or earlier until 1945, when it was given to The National Trust for Scotland. Exhibition. Garden. Disabled access to ground floor and WC.

NOTE: [Tel: 01464 831216]   Open Easter weekend; open May to September; open weekends in October. Garden and grounds open all year.

P   R   WC   £

105 Lennoxlove

Off A1, 1 mile S of Haddington, East Lothian.

Pri/LA   NT 515721   66   (Ref: H6)

Originally known as Lethington, Lennoxlove incorporates an altered L-plan tower house, which incorporates work from the 14th century, and probably earlier. A two-storey range projects from the tower, and there is another extension from the 17th century.

It was originally a property of the Giffords, but was sold to the Maitlands about 1350, who built or extended a castle here. It was burnt by the English in 1549. William Maitland of Lethington, secretary to Mary, Queen of Scots, lived here. He was involved in the plot to murder Lord Darnley, but supported Mary after she abdicated. He was taken prisoner after Edinburgh Castle was captured in 1573 and died, possibly being poisoned, soon afterwards.

The property passed to the Maitland Duke of Lauderdale in 1645, but was sold to the Stewart Lord Blantyre, from whom it passed to the Bairds. In 1947 it passed to the Duke of Hamilton, since when it has been the family seat. Among the items housed here are the death mask of

Mary, Queen of Scots, and the casket which may have contained the 'Casket Letters'. Collections of Stewart portraits and mementoes. Disabled access to gardens and WC.

NOTE: [Tel: 01620 823720]   Open Easter to end October Saturday, Sunday & Wednesday afternoons 2.00-4.30pm

P   R   WC   £

106 Linlithgow Palace

Off A803, Linlithgow, West Lothian.
HS   NT 003774   65   (Ref: H5)

Once a splendid palace and still a spectacular ruin, Linlithgow Palace consists of ranges of buildings set around a rectangular courtyard, and may include 12th-century work. Stairtowers, within the courtyard, lead to all floors and the battlements, which run all round. There is a fine carved fountain in the courtyard.

There was a 12th-century castle here, known as the Peel of Linlithgow. It was captured and strengthened by Edward I of England in 1301 during the Wars of Independence. It was slighted, after being retaken by the Scots by driving a cart under the portcullis, and remained a ruin until about 1350. It was repaired by David II, then mostly rebuilt by James I at the beginning of the 15th century. It became a favourite residence of the monarchs of Scots, and the work continued under James III and James IV. Mary, Queen of Scots, was born here in 1542.

After the Union of the Crowns in 1603, the palace was left in charge of a keeper. It was last used by Charles I in 1633 although his son, James, Duke of York, stayed here before succeeding to the throne in 1685. In the 1650s Cromwell had garrisoned the palace. In 1746 General Hawley retreated here after being defeated by the Jacobites at the Battle of Falkirk. The soldiers started fires to dry themselves, and the palace was accidentally set ablaze. It was never restored. Limited disabled access.

The palace is said to be haunted by a 'Blue Lady', which walks from the entrance of the palace to the door of the nearby parish church of St Michael. The spirit of Mary of Guise, wife of James V, reputedly haunts Queen Margaret's bower at the top of one of the stairtowers.

NOTE: [Tel: 01506 842896] Open daily all year.

P S WC £

107 Loch Doon Castle

Off A713, 7 miles S of Dalmellington, Ayrshire.

HS NX 483950 77 (Ref: I4)

Loch Doon Castle is a ruined 13th-century courtyard castle, polygonal in plan, which formerly enclosed ranges of buildings, including a 16th-century tower house. It originally stood on an inland in the middle of the loch, but when the water level was raised by a hydroelectric scheme, the castle was moved to its present site.

It was built by the Bruce Earls of Carrick, but was captured by the English in 1306, Sir Christopher Seton, Robert the Bruce's brother-in-law, being seized after the siege and hanged at Dumfries. The castle was retaken by the Scots by 1314. In 1333 it was one of the six strongholds which held out for David II against the Edward Balliol. The castle was abandoned in 17th century, and became ruinous.

NOTE: Open all year.

P

108 Lochleven Castle

Off B996, 1 mile E of Kinross, Perth & Kinross.

HS NO 138018 58 (Ref: G5)

Standing on an island in a picturesque loch, Lochleven Castle consists of a small ruinous 15th-century keep, rectangular in plan, standing at one corner of a 14th-century courtyard. The castle used to occupy most of the island, but the level of the loch has been lowered.

Lochleven was a royal castle from 1257, and was stormed by William Wallace after being captured by the English. The English besieged the castle in 1301, but it was relieved by Sir John Comyn before it could be captured. It was visited by Robert the Bruce. The castle was held again against Edward Balliol and the English in 1335. By the end of the 14th century, it had passed to the Douglases of Lochleven. Mary, Queen of Scots, was held here from 1567 until she escaped in 1568, during which time she signed her abdication – her ghost is said to haunt the castle. Lochleven passed to the Bruces, then the Grahams, and the Montgomerys, and was taken into State care in 1939.

NOTE: [Tel: 01786 450000 or 01388 040483] Open April to September – includes boat trip from Kinross.

P S WC £

109 Lochmaben Castle

Off B7020, 0.5 miles S of Lochmaben, Dumfriesshire.

HS NY 088812 78 (Ref: I5)

Once an important and powerful castle, Lochmaben Castle consists of a complex of very ruined buildings, dating in part from the 13th century, with a 15th-century keep and later additions. It had a strong curtain wall, and was surrounded by a moat.

An older castle, of which only a motte survives, may be where Robert the Bruce, later Robert I, King of Scots, was born. In 1298 Edward I of England chose a stronger site to build a castle. The castle was strengthened after being besieged by Robert the Bruce in 1299, and it was attacked again by the Scots in 1301. It was seized by Bruce in 1306, was recovered by the

English, but was finally surrendered to the Scots in 1314 after the Battle of Bannockburn.

It was held by the English from 1333 until 1384, when it was taken by Archibald the Grim, the Douglas Lord of Galloway. In 1542 it was where the Scottish army was mustered by James V before going on to defeat at Solway Moss. Mary, Queen of Scots, and Darnley attended a banquet here in 1565. In 1588 James VI besieged and captured the castle from the Maxwells. The castle was then abandoned and became ruinous.

NOTE: Open all year.

110 Lochranza Castle

Off A841, 10 miles N of Brodick, Arran.
HS NR 933507 69 (Ref: I13)

In a beautiful location, Lochranza Castle is a ruined L-plan tower house, much of which dates from the 14th century.

Lochranza was used as a hunting lodge by the kings of Scots, but from 1315 was a property of the Campbells, who built the first castle. James IV used it as a base to attack the MacDonald

Lords of the Isles. Cromwell garrisoned the castle in the 1650s, but it had been abandoned by the end of the 18th century.

NOTE: Key available from Post Office/local shop.

111 MacLellan's Castle

On A711, in Kirkcudbright, Galloway.
HS NX 683511 83 (Ref: J5)

MacLellan's Castle is a large ruinous 16th-century L-plan tower house. It consists of a main block and a wing, a projecting rectangular tower, and two towers in the re-entrant angle.

In 1569 Sir Thomas MacLellan of Bombie, Provost of Kirkcudbright, acquired the Franciscan Greyfriars Monastery. He demolished all but part of the church, which is now the Episcopalian

Church, and built the castle about 1582. The MacLellans abandoned the building around 1752, because of financial troubles, and it was sold. It was put into State care in 1912. Exhibition.
NOTE: [Tel: 01557 331856]   Open daily April to September.

P Nearby S WC £

112 Manderston
Off A6105, 1.5 miles E of Duns, Borders.
Pri/LA NT 810545 74 (Ref: H6)
Featuring the only silver staircase in the world, Manderston is a fine Edwardian mansion, part of which dates from the original house of 1790, when it was a property of the Homes. The house was virtually rebuilt between 1903-5 by the architect John Kinross for Sir James Miller, whose family had acquired the property in 1890. Fine interiors. Museum. Gardens.
NOTE: [Tel: 01361 883450]   Open 14 May to 27 September Thursday and Sunday 2.00-5.30pm; Bank Holiday open Monday 25 May and 31 August.

P S R WC £

113 Maxwelton House
Off A702, 2.5 miles E of Moniaive, Dumfriesshire.
Pri/LA NX 822898 78 (Ref: I5)
Maxwelton is a 17th-century tower house to which has been added a large mansion around three sides of a courtyard. The property originally belonged to the Cunninghams, who were made Earls of Glencairn in 1488, but was sold to the Laurie family in 1611. It was the home of the heroine of the song *Annie Laurie*. The Lauries sold the property in 1966, and the house is still occupied, now housing a museum. Gardens. Chapel.
NOTE: [Tel: 01848 200385]   Open last Sunday in May to end September daily except closed Saturdays.

P S R WC £

114 Mellerstain
Off A6089, 5 miles E of Earlston, Borders.
Pri/LA NT 648392 74 (H6)
Mellerstain House is a magnificent castellated mansion, which was designed by William and Robert Adam. The wings date from 1725, while the central block was not completed until 1778, and replaced an earlier building. Mellerstain was built for George Baillie of Jerviswood,

and is now owned by the Baillie-Hamiltons, Earls of Haddington. Fine gardens and interiors. Collections of paintings and furniture.

NOTE: [Tel: 01573 410225]   Open Easter weekend; 1 May to 30 September daily except Sat. from 12.30-5.00pm.

 R WC £

115 Morton Castle

Off A76, 2.5 miles NE of Thornhill, Dumfriesshire.

HS NX 891992 78 (Ref: I5)

Built on a strong site, Morton Castle consists of a ruined 15th-century keep or altered hall-house, and a triangular courtyard, although little remains of two sides.

The property originally belonged to the Adairs, but passed to Thomas Randolph early in the 14th century, then to the Earls of March, who built the existing castle. In 1459 it was acquired by the Douglases, later Earls of Morton. The castle was occupied until about 1715.

NOTE: Open all year – view from exterior.

P Nearby

116 Mount Stuart House

Off A844, 3.5 miles S of Rothesay, Bute.

Pri/LA NS 105595 63 (Ref: H4)

A fine Victorian Gothic house, Mount Stuart was designed by the Scottish architect Robert Rowand Anderson for the 3rd Marquis of Bute, and is still the seat of the Stuarts of Bute. It was built on the site of an earlier house of 1719, designed by Alexander MacGill and later William Adam, which was burnt down in 1877. Fine interiors. Collection of portraits. Gardens and grounds.

NOTE: [Tel: 01700 503877]   Open Easter weekend; then daily 11.00-4.30pm 1 May to 18 October, except closed Tuesday and Thursday.

 R WC £

117 Muness Castle

Off A968, SE end of island of Unst, Shetland.

HS HP 629012 1 (Ref: B7)

Muness Castle is a ruined 16th-century Z-plan tower house, consisting of a main block and round towers at diagonally opposite corners.

The castle was built by Lawrence Bruce of Cultmalindie, a Scottish incomer to Shetland. In 1573 he was appointed Chamberlain of the Lordship of Shetland, but his was a corrupt and repressive regime. Ill feeling developed between Bruce and Patrick Stewart, Earl of Orkney, and the Earl landed a force to besiege the castle in 1608, but then withdrew. The castle was burnt in 1627, although later restored. It was abandoned about 1750, and unroofed by 1774.

NOTE: Open all year.

118 Neidpath Castle

Off A72, 1 mile W of Peebles, Borders.

Pri/LA NT 236405 73 (Ref: H5)

Standing on a steep bank of the Tweed, Neidpath Castle is an altered L-plan keep with rounded corners and a small courtyard. The keep dates from the 14th century, but was substantially remodelled in the 16th century and again in the late 17th century.

An earlier castle here belonged to Sir Simon Fraser. He defeated the English at Roslin Moor in 1302, but was later captured and executed by the English. The property passed by marriage to the Hays in 1312. Mary, Queen of Scots, stayed at Neidpath in 1563, as did her son James VI in 1587. In 1650 Neidpath held out against Cromwell's army longer than any other stronghold south of the Forth. Cannon damaged the castle, and the garrison was eventually forced to surrender.

The castle was repaired, and in 1686 was sold to the Douglas Duke of Queensberry, but passed in 1810 to the Earl of Wemyss and March. Neidpath was used in filming of *The Bruce* and *Merlin – the Legend Begins*. Museum. Disabled access only to museum and ground floor of castle.

Neidpath is reputedly haunted by the ghost of a young woman. She fell in love with a local laird, but her father did not think the man good enough, and forbade them to marry. The girl died of a broken heart, and her ghost is said to haunt the castle.

NOTE: [Tel: 01721 720333]
Open daily from Thursday
before Easter to end
September; Sunday PM only.

P S WC £

119 Newark Castle

Off A708, 3 miles W of Selkirk, Borders.
Pri/LA NT 421294 73 (Ref: H6)

Standing in the grounds of the mansion of Bowhill, Newark Castle is a ruined 15th-century keep and courtyard, with a gatehouse and wall, sections of which survive.

The property was acquired by Archibald, Earl of Douglas, around 1423. It was kept by the Crown after the downfall of the Black Douglases in 1455, and given to Margaret of Denmark, wife of James III, in 1473. The castle was besieged by the English in 1547, and burnt in 1548. In 1645 one hundred followers of the Marquis of Montrose, captured after the Battle of Philiphaugh, were shot in the barmkin of Newark. Other prisoners, mostly women and children, were taken to the market place in Selkirk, and there also slain.

NOTE: [Tel: 01750 22204]   See Bowhill.

P S R WC £

120 Newark Castle

On A8, Port Glasgow, Renfrewshire.
HS NS 331745 63 (Ref: H4)

Standing on a spit of land into the sea, Newark Castle consists of a much-extended simple square 15th-century keep. To this was added a 16th-century gatehouse block and a large late 16th-century range, to form three sides of a courtyard. The remaining side was formerly completed by a wall.

Newark was originally a property of Danielstouns, but passed by marriage to the Maxwells of Calderwood in 1402, who built the castle. James IV was a frequent visitor. One of the family, Patrick Maxwell, was involved in the murders of Patrick Maxwell of Stanely in 1584 and the Montgomery Earl of Eglinton in 1596, during a series of feuds. The castle was abandoned as a residence early in the 18th century, and was put into State care in 1909.

NOTE: [Tel: 01745 741858] Open April to September.

P S WC £

121 Noltland Castle

Off B9066, NE side of island of Westray, Orkney.
HS HY 430487 5 (Ref: A6)

A strong and grim stronghold, Noltland Castle is a large ruined 16th-century Z-plan tower house. A later courtyard survives with the remains of a L-plan range of buildings.

An earlier castle here was held by a Thomas de Tulloch in 1420, and towards the end of the 15th century was besieged by the Sinclairs of Warsetter. The present castle was built by Gilbert Balfour, who was Master of the Household to Mary, Queen of Scots. He had been involved in the murders of Cardinal Beaton in 1546, for which he was imprisoned, and Lord Darnley in 1567. He supported Mary after she fled to England, but when her cause became hopeless he fled Scotland, and served in the Swedish army until his death by execution in 1576 after plotting against the Swedish king.

The castle was besieged and captured in 1592 by Patrick Stewart, Earl of Orkney, in order to get payment of a debt. Some of the Marquis of Montrose's men took refuge here after their defeat at Carbisdale in 1650, and the castle was later held by Cromwell's men. Noltland was abandoned about 1760.

NOTE: Open all year.

122 Orchardton Tower

Off A711, 4 miles S of Dalbeattie, Galloway.
HS NX 817551 84 (J5)
The only free-standing circular tower house in Scotland, Orchardton Tower is a ruinous round

Orchardton Tower

tower house of four storeys, dating from the 15th and 16th centuries. Foundations of courtyard buildings survive.

The lands of Orchardton were acquired by the Cairns family early in the 15th century, and they built the tower, but it later passed by marriage to the Maxwells. During the Jacobite Rising of 1745, one of the family, Sir Robert Maxwell, was wounded and captured at Culloden in 1746, and taken to Carlisle for trial and probable execution. He tried to destroy his personal papers, but was prevented, and his commission as an officer in the French army was found. He was thereafter treated as a prisoner of war, and was sent to France rather than being executed. He later returned to Orchardton.

NOTE: Open all year.

123 Paxton House

Off B6461, 4 miles W of Berwick-upon-Tweed, Borders.
Pri/LA NT 935530 74 (Ref: H7)
In a picturesque setting overlooking the Tweed, Paxton House is a fine classical mansion. It consists of a central block, with columns and two flanking wings, and was built in 1756 for the Homes of Billie. The house was probably designed by John and Robert Adam, and in 1811 a gallery and library were added to designs by Robert Reid. Paxton is now an outstation of the National Galleries of Scotland. Exhibitions of pictures and furniture. Gardens, woodlands and parkland. Partial disabled access to house.

NOTE: [Tel: 01289 386291] House open daily 11.00am-4.15pm; grounds daily 10.00am to sunset. Good Friday to October.

124 Peel Ring of Lumphanan

Off A93, 5 miles NE of Aboyne, Kincardine & Deeside.
HS NJ 576037 37 (Ref: E6)
Site of 12th-century castle of enclosure, now consisting of a large but low motte with a ditch. It was held by the Durwards in the 13th century, and visited by Edward I of England in 1296. There are some remains of a building occupied until 1782.

NOTE: Open all year.

125 Provost Skene's House

Off A92, 45 Guest Row, Broad Street, Aberdeen.
Pri/LA NJ 943064 38 (Ref: E7)
Provost Skene's House is a fine 16th-century fortified town house. A magnificent 17th-century plaster ceiling and wood panelling survives, and the painted gallery houses a good collection of religious paintings. Other rooms include a suite of Georgian chambers, and an Edwardian nursery.

NOTE: [Tel: 01224 646333] Open daily all year Monday to Saturday except 25/ 26 December and 1/2 January.

P Nearby S R WC

126 Queen Mary's House, Jedburgh

Off A68, in Jedburgh, Borders.

Pri/LA NT 651206 74 (Ref: H6)

Situated in a public park, Queen Mary's House is an altered 16th-century T-plan tower house,

consisting of a main block and a centrally projecting wing. A vaulted pend led to a courtyard, little of which remains.

The house belonged to the of Scotts of Ancrum. Mary, Queen of Scots, stayed in a chamber on the second floor. She was ill and lay near death for many days after her visit to the Earl of Bothwell at Hermitage Castle in 1566.

The building houses a museum displaying exhibits relating to the visit by Mary to Jedburgh. Award winning visitor centre.

NOTE: [Tel: 01835 863331] Open 1 March to end November.

P Nearby S WC £

127 Ravenscraig Castle

Off A955, 1 mile NE of Kirkcaldy, Fife.

HS NT 291925 59 (Ref: G6)

Ravenscraig Castle is a ruinous altered 15th-century castle and courtyard, and one of the first castles in Scotland built to withstand and return artillery fire. It consists of two D-plan towers, with very thick walls, and a courtyard cut off from the mainland by a deep ditch. The towers were linked by a two-storey block with a broad parapet.

James II, who died when a cannon exploded during the siege of Roxburgh Castle, started to build Ravenscraig before 1460 for Mary of Gueldres. She died at the castle in 1463. It was forced upon William Sinclair, then Earl of Orkney, by James III in return for Kirkwall Castle, on Orkney, which the King wanted for himself. The Sinclairs held the property until 1898, and it was taken into State care in 1955. Only part of the building is now accessible.

NOTE: Open all year.

P

128 Rothesay Castle

Off A886, in Rothesay, Bute.

HS NS 086646 63 (Ref: H4)

Surrounded by a wet moat and built on a mound or motte, Rothesay Castle consists of an enormous 12th-century shell keep, with four round towers. In the late 15th century a large

rectangular keep and gatehouse were added.

The castle was attacked by Norsemen in the 1230s, who cut a hole in the wall with their axes. It was captured in 1263 by King Haakon of Norway, before he was defeated at the Battle of Largs. The Stewarts were keepers of the castle. Rothesay was held by the English during the Wars of Independence, but was taken by Robert the Bruce, only to be captured again by the English in 1334, once again to be recaptured by the Scots.

It was a favourite residence of Robert II and Robert III, who may have died here rather than at Dundonald in 1406. In 1401 Robert III made his son Duke of Rothesay, a title since taken by the eldest son of the kings of Scots and currently held by Prince Charles. The castle was besieged by the Earl of Ross in 1462, the Master of Ruthven in 1527, and in 1544 was captured by the Earl of Lennox on behalf of the English. In the 1650s it was held for Charles I, but later taken by Cromwell, whose men damaged the castle. Argyll's forces torched the castle in 1685, and it was ruinous until in 1816 when part was repaired. It was put into the care of the State in 1961. Exhibition.

NOTE: [Tel: 01700 502691] Open daily all year except closed Thursday PM and Fridays October to March.

P Nearby   S   WC   £

129 Ruthven Barracks

Off A9, 1 mile S of Kingussie, Highland.

HS NN 764997 35 (Ref: E5)

Nothing remains, except substantial earthworks, of a 13th-century castle of the Comyns, later held by Alexander Stewart, the Wolf of Badenoch, as the chief stronghold of his lordship. In 1451 the castle passed to the Gordon, Earl of Huntly, but in that year it was sacked by John MacDonald, Earl of Ross. It was rebuilt by 1459 when James II visited. Mary, Queen of Scots stayed at the castle. It was twice damaged by fire, and in 1689 attacked by Jacobites.

In 1718 the castle was demolished and replaced by a barracks, for Hanoverian troops, on the earthworks of the old castle. It was held by government forces in 1746, but was eventually

taken and burnt by Jacobite forces. It was not restored, and the buildings are ruinous.
NOTE: Open all year.

P

130 Scalloway Castle

Off A970, in Scalloway, Shetland.
HS HU 404392 4 (Ref: C7)
Scalloway Castle is a ruinous 17th-century L-plan tower house, consisting of a main block and a smaller square offset wing.

The castle was built by Patrick Stewart, Earl of Orkney, in 1600. He was unpopular with both the Orcadians and the folk of Shetland, forcing local people to work on the castle and taxing them to pay for materials. Earl Patrick was executed in 1615. The castle was occupied by Cromwell's forces in the 1650s, and was abandoned by the end of the 17th century. In 1908 the castle was given over to the State, and the vaults were repaired or rebuilt. Exhibition.
NOTE: Open all year.

P Nearby

131 Scone Palace

Off A93, N of Perth.
Pri/LA NO 114267 58 (Ref: G5)
Scone Palace, a large castellated mansion dating from 1802 and designed by William Atkinson, incorporates part of the palace built by the Ruthvens in the 1580s, itself probably created out of the Abbot's Lodging.

Scone was a centre of the Picts, and in the 6th century a Culdee cell of the early Celtic church was founded here. The Kings of Scots were inaugurated at the Moot Hill, near the present palace, from the reign of Kenneth MacAlpin. An abbey was founded here in the 12th century, and the 'Stone of Destiny', also called the Stone of Scone, was kept here, until taken to Westminster Abbey by Edward I in 1296 – although this was returned to Edinburgh Castle in 1996. The last king to be inaugurated here was Charles II in 1651.

The abbey was sacked by a Reforming mob in 1559, and there are no remains. The property passed to the Ruthvens in 1580. However, after the 'Gowrie Conspiracy' in 1600, when the Ruthven Earl of Gowrie and his brother, the Master of Ruthven, were murdered by James VI and others, Scone passed to the Murrays, as David Murray of Gospertie had been one of those to save the King's life. The family were made Viscounts Stormont in 1602, and Earls of Mansfield in 1776. Fine collections of furniture, clocks, needlework and porcelain. Gardens. Limited disabled access and WC.

The old village of Scone was moved in 1804-5 to New Scone, as it was too close to the Palace for the then owners.
NOTE: [Tel: 01738 552300] Open daily Easter to 2nd Monday October.

P S R WC £

132 Scotstarvit Tower

Off A916, 2 miles S of Cupar, Fife.
NTS NO 370113 59 (Ref: G6)
A fine and well-preserved building, Scotstarvit Tower is a 16th-century L-plan tower house, and was originally a property of the Inglis family, but was sold to the Scotts in 1611. Sir John Scott of Scotstarvit was an eminent historian. The property was sold to the Gourlays of Craigrothie about 1780, then to the Wemyss family, then to the Sharps in 1904. It was given to

the National Trust for Scotland in 1949 – see Hill of Tarvit.

NOTE: [Tel: 01334 653127] Administered by Historic Scotland. Key available at Hill of Tarvit, which is open Easter, May to September, weekends in October.

P S R WC £

133 Shambellie House Museum of Costume

Off A710, New Abbey, 7 miles S of Dumfries.

Pri/LA NX 960665 84 (Ref: I5)

Situated in a Victorian house set in mature woodlands, each year the museum exhibits a new display of European fashionable dress from the National Costume Collection.

NOTE: [Tel: 01387 850375] Open daily 1 April to 31 October 11.00-5.00pm.

P S R WC £

134 Skipness Castle

Off B8001, 7 miles S of Tarbert, Argyll.

HS NR 907577 62 (Ref: H3)

Skipness Castle is a ruinous 13th-century castle of enclosure, consisting of a courtyard with a curtain wall surrounding a tower house and ranges of buildings. The wall has three ruined towers. The main entrance was from the sea, which was defended by a gatetower, with a portcullis and machiolation.

The first castle was probably built by the MacSweens around 1247, and it was strengthened against the Norsemen about 1262. It was held by the MacDonald Lords of the Isles until 1493, when they were forfeited. The castle was then granted to the Forresters, but in 1499 it was acquired by the Campbell Earl of Argyll. It was besieged unsuccessfully by Alaisdair Colkitto MacDonald in the 1640s, but was abandoned at the end of the 17th century.

There are the ruins of a chapel, dedicated to St Brendan, south-east of the castle.

NOTE: Open all year.

P

135 Smailholm Tower

Off B6397, 5 miles W of Kelso, Borders.

HS NT 637346 74 (Ref: H6)

Standing on a rocky hillock, Smailholm Tower is a plain 15th-century tower house, rectangular in plan. It stood in a small walled courtyard, which enclosed ranges of buildings, including a chapel and kitchen.

It was a property of the Pringle family from 1408. David Pringle of Smailholm was killed, together with his four sons, at the Battle of Flodden in 1513. The tower was attacked by the English in 1543, and again in 1546, when the garrison of Wark made off with 60 cattle and four prisoners. The property was sold to the Scotts of Harden in 1645, but the tower was abandoned about 1700. The tower houses an exhibition of dolls illustrating some of the Border ballads.

NOTE: [Tel: 01573 460365] Open April to September.

P S £

136 Spynie Palace

Off A941, 2.5 miles N of Elgin, Moray.

HS NJ 231658 28 (Ref: D5)

One of the finest castles in Scotland, Spynie Palace consists of a massive 15th-century keep, Davy's Tower, at one corner of a large courtyard, enclosed by a wall, with square corner towers.

In one wall is a gatehouse, and there were ranges of buildings, including a chapel, within the courtyard walls. All are now ruinous.

In 1200 Bishop Richard moved the cathedral of Moray to Spynie, where it stayed for 24 years, and although the cathedral was moved back to Elgin, the Bishops kept their residence and stronghold here. The palace was probably built by Bishop Innes, after Elgin Cathedral had been burnt by Alexander Stewart, the Wolf of Badenoch. Bishop David Stewart, who died in 1475, excommunicated the Gordon Earl of Huntly, and built the great keep, Davy's Tower, to defend himself against Huntly. James IV visited the palace in 1493 and in 1505, as did Mary, Queen of Scots in 1562.

After the Reformation the palace was used by Protestant Bishops. James VI stayed here in 1589. General Munro besieged the castle in 1640, and compelled Bishop Guthrie to surrender it, and the Bishop was imprisoned. The last resident Bishop was Colin Falconer, who died here in 1686, and Bishop Hay, the last Bishop, was removed from office in 1688. The building then became ruinous.

NOTE: [Tel: 01343 546358]   Open daily April to September but weekends only October to March. Joint ticket with Elgin Cathedral.

P S WC £

137 St Andrews Castle

Off A91, in St Andrews, Fife.

HS NO 513169 59 (Ref: G6)

Standing close to the remains of the large cathedral, St Andrews Castle is a ruined courtyard castle, enclosed by a wall. There was a gatehouse and towers at the corners, one of which contained a bottle dungeon cut into the rock. Much of the castle is very ruined.

The first castle here was built by Bishop Roger, but was dismantled by Robert the Bruce around 1310. It was rebuilt in 1336 by the English in support of Edward Balliol, but was captured by Sir Andrew Moray in 1337, and slighted again. At the end of the 14th century, Bishop Trail rebuilt the castle.

Cardinal David Beaton strengthened the castle by adding two round blockhouses, now destroyed. In 1546 a band of Protestants murdered Beaton in the castle, and hung his naked body from one of the tower. Reinforced by others, including John Knox, they held the castle for a year. The besiegers tunnelled towards the walls, and the defenders countermined and captured their tunnel. Both tunnels still survive. It was only with the arrival of a French fleet that the garrison surrendered and became galley slaves, John Knox among them.

The castle was restored to the new Protestant bishops in 1612. However, the castle had lost its importance, and by 1654 the town council had stone removed from the castle to repair the harbour. Exhibition and visitor centre. Reasonable disabled access and WC.

NOTE: [Tel: 01334 477196]   Open all year – a combined ticket for cathedral & castle is available.

P Nearby   S   WC   £

138 Stirling Castle
Off A872, in Stirling.
HS   NS 790940   57   (Ref: G5)
One of the most important and powerful castles in Scotland, Stirling Castle stands on a high rock, and consists of a courtyard castle, which dates in part from the 12th century. The castle is entered through the 18th-century outer defences and 16th-century forework of which the Prince's Tower and the gatehouse survive, but the Elphinstone Tower has been reduced to its base. The gatehouse leads to the Lower Square, which is bordered on one side by the King's Old Building, and on another by the gable of the Great Hall. A road leads between the King's Old Buildings and the hall to the Upper Square. The Chapel Royal is built on one side of the square, as is the Great Hall, which was completed during the reign of James IV. Other features of interest are the kitchens, the wall walk and the nearby 'King's Knot', an ornamental garden, which once had a pleasure canal.

The earliest recorded castle at Stirling was used by Malcolm Canmore in the 11th century. Alexander I died here in 1124, as did William the Lyon in 1214. Edward I of England captured the castle in 1304 when he used – although after the garrison had surrendered – a siege engine called the 'War Wolf'. William Wallace took the castle for the Scots, but it was retaken by the English until the Battle of Bannockburn in 1314.

Robert the Bruce had the castle slighted, but it was rebuilt by Edward III of England, after his victory of Halidon Hill in 1333, in support of Edward Balliol. The English garrison was besieged in 1337 by Andrew Moray, but it was not until 1342 that the Scots recovered the castle.

James III was born here in 1451. James II lured the 8th Earl of Douglas to it in 1452, murdered him, and had his body tossed out of one of the windows, despite promising safe conduct. Mary, Queen of Scots, was crowned in the old chapel in 1543, and the future James VI was baptised here in 1566. James VI stayed here in 1617, as did Charles I in 1633, and Charles II in 1650. In 1651 the castle was besieged by Monck for Cromwell, but it surrendered after a few days after a mutiny by the garrison.

It was in a poor state of repair in the 18th century, but the garrison harried the Jacobites during both the 1715 and 1745 Risings. After 1745, the castle was subdivided to be used as a barracks, but the army left in 1964. Exhibition of life in the royal palace, introductory display, medieval kitchen display. Limited disabled access and WC.

NOTE: [Tel: 01786 450000]   Open all year. Joint ticket with Argyll's Lodging.

P   S   R   WC   £

139 Stranraer Castle

Off A77, Stranraer, Galloway.

Pri/LA NX 061608 82 (Ref: J4)

Stranraer Castle, also known as Castle of St John, is a much-altered 16th-century L-plan tower house, probably built by Adair of Kilhilt around 1511, although it may be older. It passed to the Kennedys of Chappel before 1596, then in 1680 to the Dalrymples of Stair. John Graham of Claverhouse, 'Bloody Clavers', stayed here while suppressing Covenanters from 1682-5 as one of his duties as the Sheriff of Galloway. The castle is now a museum, with exhibitions telling the history from its building to its use in the 19th century as a town jail.

NOTE: [Tel: 01776 705088/705544]   Open Easter to mid-September 10.00am-1.00pm and 2.00-5.00pm; closed Sunday.

P Nearby S £

140 Tantallon Castle

Off A198, 3 miles E of North Berwick, East Lothian.

HS NT 596851 67 (Ref: H6)

One of the most impressive castles in southern Scotland, Tantallon Castle is a large and once strong 14th-century courtyard castle, now ruinous. It consists of a massively thick 50-foot-high

curtain wall, blocking off a high promontory, the sea and the height of the cliffs defending the three other sides. In front of the wall is a deep ditch, and at each end are ruined towers: one round, one D-shaped. The shell of a massive keep-gatehouse stands at the middle of the wall, and rises to six storeys. Within the castle walls are the remains of a range of buildings, which contained a hall and private chambers.

The castle was built by William Douglas, 1st Earl of Douglas, about 1350. William waylaid and slew his godfather, another William Douglas, the infamous 'Knight of Liddelsdale', and secured his position as the most powerful lord in the Borders. George Douglas, his son, became the

1st Earl of Angus, the first of the 'Red Douglases'.

Archibald, the 5th Earl, known as 'Bell-the-Cat', hanged James III's favourites, including Cochrane, from the bridge at Lauder. He entered into a treasonable pact with Henry VII of England, which led to James IV besieging Tantallon. In 1513 Douglas died, and his two sons were killed at the Battle of Flodden. The castle was attacked again in 1528 by James V; and Mary, Queen of Scots, visited in 1566. In 1651 Cromwell sent an army to seize the castle, as men from Tantallon, as well as Dirleton, had been attacking his lines of communication. The bombardment had lasted only 12 days when the garrison surrendered. The castle was damaged and became ruinous, and was sold to the Dalrymples in 1699. It was taken into the care of the State in 1924. Short walk to castle. Exhibition.

NOTE: [Tel: 01620 892727] Open daily all year except closed Thursday PM and Fridays October to March.

```
P  S  R  WC  £
```

141 The Binns

Off A904, 3 miles NE of Linlithgow, West Lothian.
NTS NT 051785 65 (Ref: H5)
The Binns, a fine castellated mansion, was built between 1612 and 1630, with additions and remodelling later in the 17th century, in the 1740s, and the 1820s. It has fine plaster ceilings from the 17th century; and incorporates part of an old castle.

It was a property of the Livingstones of Kilsyth, but was sold to the Dalziels in 1612. General Tom Dalziel of The Binns was taken prisoner in 1651 at the Battle of Worcester – when in an army under Charles II, which was defeated by Cromwell – but escaped from the Tower of London, and joined the Royalist rising of 1654. He went into exile when the rising collapsed, and served in the Russian army with the Tsar's Cossacks, when he is reputed to have roasted prisoners. Returning after the Restoration, Dalziel was made commander of forces in Scotland from 1666 to 1685. He led the force that defeated the Covenanters at the Battle of Rullion Green in 1666.

The house was presented to The National Trust for Scotland in 1944. Collections of portraits, furniture and china. Grounds. Limited disabled access and WC.

NOTE: [Tel: 01506 834255] Open daily May to September, except Fridays. Parkland open all year.

```
P  WC  £              o
```

142 Thirlestane Castle

Off A68, NE of Lauder, Borders.
Pri/LA NT 534479 73 (Ref: H6)
Thirlestane Castle consists of a rectangular tower house or block, dating from the 16th century, which was considerably enlarged in the 1670s by the architect William Bruce. A symmetrical forecourt with wings was also added, and these were extended in the 19th century by David Bryce. A fine 17th-century plaster ceiling survives on the second floor, as do Baroque plaster ceilings elsewhere.

A castle, called Lauder Fort, was built here by Edward I of England, during the Wars of Independence. It was strengthened by Protector Somerset and the English in 1548, although it was retaken by the Scots, with French help, by 1550.

The present castle was started by Sir John Maitland, James VI's chancellor, but it was John Maitland, Duke of Lauderdale, a very powerful man in Scotland in the 17th century, who had it remodelled as it is today. Bonnie Prince Charlie stayed here in 1745. The castle is still occupied by the Dukes of Lauderdale. Collection of portraits, furniture and china. Exhibition of historical toys and Border country life.

NOTE: [Tel: 01578 722430]   Open Monday, Wednesday, Thursday & Sunday Easter-week, May, June & September PM; Open Sunday to Friday July & August PM.

P S R WC £

143 Threave Castle

Off A75, 3 miles W of Castle Douglas, Galloway.
NTS NX 739623 84 (Ref: J5)

Threave Castle consists of a massive 14th-century keep, rectangular in plan, which stood within a courtyard, enclosed by a wall and ditch, with drum towers at each corner, only one of which survives.

An earlier castle here was burnt by Edward Bruce in 1308. The present castle was started by Archibald the Grim – so named because his face was terrible to look upon in battle – 3rd Earl of Douglas, and Lord of Galloway from 1369. He died at Threave in 1400.

It was from Threave that the young 6th Earl and his brother rode to Edinburgh Castle in 1440 for the 'Black Dinner', where both were taken out and executed. The 8th Earl was murdered

in 1452 by James II at Stirling, after being invited there as an act of reconciliation. In 1455 James II bombarded Threave with artillery, including – it is said – the cannon 'Mons Meg' to dislodge the Douglases. The garrison surrendered, but this seems to have been achieved by bribery .

In 1640 the castle was attacked by an army of Covenanters for 13 weeks until forced to surrender. The castle was slighted and partly dismantled. It was given to The National Trust of Scotland in 1948.

NOTE: [Tel: 01831 168512]   Open daily April to September. Administered by Historic Scotland – includes long walk and short ferry trip.

P S WC £

144 Tolquhon Castle

Off A999, 4 miles E of Oldmeldrum, Aberdeenshire.

HS NJ 873286 38 (Ref: D6)

Once a strong but comfortable fortress, Tolquhon Castle consists of a ruined 15th-century keep in one corner of a courtyard, enclosed by ranges of buildings, including a drum-towered gatehouse.

The original keep was built by the Prestons of Craigmillar, but the property passed by marriage to the Forbes family in 1420, who built the rest of the castle. The 6th Laird died at the Battle of Pinkie in 1547. James VI visited in 1589, while the 10th laird saved Charles II's life at the Battle of Worcester in 1651.

The Forbes sold the property to the Farquhars in 1716, although the 11th Forbes laird had to be forcibly removed from the castle. The building was used as a farmhouse, but was abandoned and became ruinous. It was put into the care of the State in 1929. Reasonable disabled access and WC.

NOTE: [Tel: 01651 851286] Open April to September and weekends only October to March.

P S WC £

145 Torosay Castle

On A849, 1.5 miles SE of Craignure, Mull.

Pri/LA NM 729353 49 (Ref: G3)

Torosay Castle is a castellated mansion of 1858, designed by the architect David Bryce for the Campbells of Possel. It was sold to the Guthrie family in 1865, and remains with their descendants. The gardens, laid out by Sir Robert Lorimer in 1899, include formal terraces, an Italian statue walk, and woodland. Miniature steam railway from Craignure. Disabled access to grounds; WC.

NOTE: [Tel: 01680 812421] Open daily 10.30am to 5.30pm Easter to October; gardens open all year.

P S R WC £

146 Traquair House

Off B709, 1 mile S of Innerleithen, Borders.

Pri/LA NT 330354 73 (Ref: H6)

Said to be one of the oldest continuously inhabited houses in Scotland, Traquair House is an altered and extended tower house, which may incorporate work from as early as the 12th century.

Alexander I had a hunting lodge here, but the lands had passed to the Douglases by the 13th century, then through several families until sold to the Stewart Earls of Buchan in 1478. Mary, Queen of Scots, visited with Lord Darnley in 1566. She left behind a quilt, possibly embroidered by herself and her four Marys.

Bonnie Prince Charlie stayed in the house in 1745, entering through the Bear Gates. One story is that the 5th Earl closed and locked them after Charlie's departure, swearing they would not be unlocked until a Stewart once more sat on the throne of the country. They are still locked. The house has a collection of Stewart mementoes. Working 18th-century brewery.

Gardens and maze. Craft workshops. Gift and Cashmere shop.

NOTE: [Tel: 01896 830323] Open daily Easter to September; open Friday, Saturday and Sunday only in October.

`P S R WC £`

147 Urquhart Castle

Off A82, 1.5 miles E of Drumnadrochit, Highland.

HS NH 531286 26 (Ref: D4)

Standing in a picturesque location on the shore of Loch Ness, Urquhart Castle consists of a 13th-century castle of enclosure with a curtain wall and gatehouse. The courtyard encloses ranges of buildings, including a hall and chapel, and has a 16th-century tower house at one end. The buildings are ruinous.

The Picts had a fort here in the 6th century, which St Columba may have visited. The castle was held by the Durwards in the mid 13th century, but passed to the Comyns. It was taken in 1296 by the English, was retaken by the Scots, only to be recaptured by the English in 1303. In 1308 it was besieged again by the Scots, led by Robert the Bruce, and taken for the Scots.

The castle held out for David II in 1333 against Edward Balliol and Edward III of England. It was captured in 1437 by the Earl of Ross; in 1515 by the MacDonalds; and in 1545 by the MacDonalds and Camerons. In 1644 the castle was sacked by Covenanters. The castle held out against the Jacobites in 1689, but was dismantled in 1691 when the gatehouse was destroyed with gunpowder.

There have been many sightings of the Loch Ness Monster from near the castle – and there are two monster exhibition centres in nearby Drumnadrochit.

NOTE: [Tel: 01456 450551] Open all year – walk to castle.

`P S WC £`

Some other sites open to the public

148 Arbuthnott House, Laurencekirk [01561 361226] Garden open all year; house: tel to confirm.

149 Arniston House, Gorebridge, Midlothian [01875 830515] Open Jul to mid-Sep Sun, Tue & Thu PM.

150 Balfour Castle, Shapinsay, Orkney [01856 711282] Open mid-May to mid-Sep Wed & Sun.

151 Balnain House, Huntly Street, Inverness [01463 715757] Open all year – tel to confirm.

152 Broughton House & Garden, High Street, Kirkcudbright [01557 330437] Open daily Apr to Oct.

153 Carlyle's Birthplace, Ecclefechan, Dumfriesshire [01576 300666] Open May to Sep Fri to Mon.

154 Carsluith Castle, Carsluith, Galloway Open all year.

155 Castle Kennedy Gardens, near Stranraer, Galloway [01776 702024] Open daily Apr to Sep.

156 Castle Stuart, Petty, Inverness [01463 790745] Open daily May to Oct.

157 Charleton House, Colinsburgh, Fife [01333 340249] Open Sep guided tours.

158 Chatelherault Hunting Lodge, Hamilton [01698 426213] Open all year.

159 Colzium House & Walled Garden, Kilsyth [01236 823821] Grdn daily Easter to Sep; wknds winter.

160 Comlongon Castle, Clarencefield, Dumfriesshire [01387 870283] By appointment.

161 Corehouse, Lanark [01555 663126] Open Aug to mid-Sep guided tours.

162 Coxton Tower, nr Elgin, Moray [01343 842225] By appointment.

163 Craigdarroch House, Moniaive, Dumfriesshire [01848 200202] Open daily Jul 2.00-4.00pm.

164 Craigston Castle, Turriff, Aberdeenshire [01888 551228] Jul to Aug lim opening – tel to confirm.

165 Dalkeith Park, Dalkeith, Midlothian [0131 663 5684] Open daily Mar to Oct.

166 Dalmeny House, South Queensferry, Edinburgh [0131 331 1888] Open Jul/Aug Sun, Mon & Tue PM.

167 Darnaway Castle, Forres, Moray [01309 641469] By appointment.

168 Drummuir Castle, Keith, Banffshire [01542 810332] Limited opening Sep – tel to confirm.

169 Georgian House, Charlotte Square, Edinburgh [0131 226 3318] Open daily Apr to Oct.

170 Gladstone's Land, Royal Mile, Edinburgh [0131 226 5856] Open daily Apr to Oct.

171 Gosford House, Longniddry, East Lothian [01875 870201] Open Jun/Jul Wed, Sat & Sun PM.

172 Halliwell's House Museum, Selkirk, Borders [01750 20096] Open daily Easter to Oct.

173 The Hirsel Country Park and Museum, Coldstream, Borders [01890 882834] Park open all year.

174 Holmwood House, Netherlee Road, Cathcart, Glasgow [0141 637 2129] Open daily end-Aug to Oct.

175 Hutchesons' Hall, Ingram Street, Glasgow [0141 552 8391] Open all year excpt BHs & Sun.

176 Inveresk Lodge Garden, Musselburgh, East Lothian [01721 722502] Open all year clsd Sat winter.

177 Malleny Garden, Balerno, Edinburgh [0131 449 2283] Open daily all year.

178 Megginch Castle Gardens, Errol, Perthshire [01821 642222] Open Wed Apr to Oct; daily Aug.

179 Menstrie Castle, Castle Road, Menstrie, Clackmannan [01259 213131] Open Easter wknd, then May to Sep Sat & Sun.

180 Minard Castle, Crieff, Perthshire [01546 886272] By appointment.

181 Monzie Castle, Crieff, Perthshire [01764 653110] Open mid-May to mid-Jun PM & by appointment.

182 Mugdock Country Park, Milngavie [0141 956 6100] Open all year.

183 Newliston, Kirkliston, West Lothian [0131 333 3231] Open May Wed to Sun PM, & by appointment.

184 Old Gala House, Galashiels, Borders [01750 20096] Open daily Tue to Sat late Mar to early Nov.

185 Parliament House, Royal Mile, Edinburgh [0131 225 2595] Open all year Mon to Fri.

186 Pitmedden Garden, Ellon, Aberdeenshire [01651 842352] Open daily May to September.

187 Pollok House and Country Park, Glasgow [0141 649 7151] Open summer; tel to confirm.

188 Preston Tower, Prestonpans, East Lothian [0131 226 5922] Open all year.

189 Provan Hall, Easterhouse, Glasgow [0141 771 4399] Open all year – tel to confirm.

190 Provost Ross's House, Shiprow, Aberdeen [01224 210804] Open all year.

191 Rammerscales, Lockerbie, Dumfriesshire [01387 810229] Open Jul/Aug; tel to confirm.

192 Sorn Castle, Ayrshire [01290 268181] By appointment.

193 Stevenson House, Haddington, East Lothian [01620 823217] Open Jul daily excpt Fri & by apptmnt.

194 Strome Castle, Lochcarron, Highland Open all year.

195 Tankerness House, Broad Street, Kirkwall, Orkney [01856 873191] Open daily all year.

196 Towie Barclay Castle, Aberdeenshire [01888 511347] By appointment.

197 Winton House, Pencaitland, East Lothian [01620 824986] By appointment.

Glossary

Angle-Turret Turret crowning corner of a building

Arcade A series of arches supported by columns

Arch A self-supporting structure capable of carrying a load over an opening

Attic The top storey entirely within a gabled roof

Bailey A defensible area enclosed by a wall or palisade and a ditch

Bartizan Turret crowning corner of a building

Basement The lowest storey of a building, sometimes below ground level

Battlement A crenellated parapet to shoot between the solid sections

Caphouse A small watch-chamber at the top of a turnpike stair, often opening into the parapet walk

Castle A stronghold, residence of a nobleman or landowner

Castellations Battlements and turrets

Corbiestepped *(Scots)* Squared stones forming steps upon a gable

Corbel A projecting bracket supporting other stonework or timbers

Courtyard castle Usually a castle of some size and importance built around a central courtyard, with a tower or keep, gatehouse, and ranges of buildings

Crenellations Battlements

Crowstepped Squared stones forming steps upon a gable (corbiestepped)

Curtain Wall A high enclosing stone wall around a bailey

E-plan tower house Tower house with a main block and at least two wings at right angles, dating from the 16th and 17th centuries

Enceinte The line of the wall encircling a fortress

Gable A vertical wall or other vertical surface, frequently triangular, at the end of a pitched roof. In Scotland often corbiestepped

Gallery A balcony or passage, often with seats, usually overlooking a great hall or garden

Garret The top storey of a building within the roof

Keep Strong stone tower. A citadel or ultimate strong point, normally with a vaulted basement, hall and additional storeys. Originally called a donjon

L-plan tower house Distinctive Scottish form of the tower house in which a wing was added at right angles to the main tower block

Main Block Principal part of a castle, usually containing the hall and lord's chamber

Moat A ditch, water filled or dry, around an enclosure

Motte A steeply sided flat-topped mound

Motte and bailey A defence system, Roman in origin, consisting of an earth motte (mound) carrying a wooden tower with a bailey (open court) with an enclosing ditch and palisade

Palace An old Scottish term for a two-storey hall block

Parapet A wall for protection at any sudden drop, but defensive in a castle

Pit-Prison A dark prison only reached by a hatch in a vault

Portcullis A wooden and/or iron gate designed to rise and fall in vertical grooves

Postern A secondary gateway or doorway; a back entrance

Rampart A stone or earth wall surrounding a stronghold

Royal castle A castle held by a keeper or constable for the monarch

Scale-and-platt Stair with short straight flights and turnings at landings

Slight To destroy a castle's defences

Tempera Form of wall painting directly onto wet plaster

Tower House Self-contained house with the main rooms stacked vertically usually with a hall over a vaulted basement with further storeys above

T-plan House or tower where the main (long) block has a wing or tower (usually for the stair) in the centre of one front

Turnpike stair Spiral stair around a newel or central post

Turret A small tower usually attached to a building

Vault An arched ceiling of stone

Yett A strong hinged gate made of interwoven iron bars

Walled Enclosure A simple castle, normally where a wall encloses a rock or island with a wooden hall and buildings

Z-plan Distinctive Scottish form of the tower house where two corner towers were added to the main tower block at diagonally opposite corners

Index

Index